D1624580

Mandatory
Military Service

American Military Policy
Capital Punishment
Election Reform
Freedom of Speech
Gun Control
Legalizing Marijuana
Mandatory Military Service
Mental Health Reform
Physician-Assisted Suicide
Religion in Public Schools
The Right to Privacy
Trial of Juveniles as Adults

Mandatory Military Service

Paul Ruschmann, J.D.

SERIES CONSULTING EDITOR
Alan Marzilli, M.A., J.D.

CHELSEA HOUSE
P U B L I S H E R S
A Haights Cross Communications Company

Philadelphia

CHELSEA HOUSE PUBLISHERS

VP, NEW PRODUCT DEVELOPMENT Sally Cheney
DIRECTOR OF PRODUCTION Kim Shinners
CREATIVE MANAGER Takeshi Takahashi
MANUFACTURING MANAGER Diann Grasse

Staff for MANDATORY MILITARY SERVICE

EXECUTIVE EDITOR Lee Marcott
SENIOR EDITOR Tara Koellhoffer
PRODUCTION EDITOR Megan Emery
ASSISTANT PHOTO EDITOR Noelle Nardone
SERIES AND COVER DESIGNER Keith Trego
LAYOUT 21st Century Publishing and Communications, Inc.

A Haights Cross Communications ◀ Company

http://www.chelseahouse.com

First Printing

1 3 5 7 9 8 6 4 2

Library of Congress Cataloging-in-Publication Data

Ruschmann, Paul.
  Mandatory military service / Paul Ruschmann.
      p. cm. -- (Point-counterpoint)
  Includes index.
  Contents: History of the draft -- Point: an all-volunteer military
service endangers national security -- Counterpoint: the United States
can meet its military commitments without a draft -- Point: reviving
the draft would benefit society -- Counterpoint: reviving the draft
would do more harm than good -- Point: even without a draft, a national
service requirement would benefit society -- Counterpoint: a national
service requirement is unnecessary and unfair -- The future of
mandatory service.
  ISBN 0-7910-7919-8
  1. Draft--United States--Juvenile literature. [1. Draft. 2. National
security.] I. Title. II. Point-counterpoint (Philadelphia, Pa.) III.
Series.
  UB343.R87 2003
  355.2'2363'0973--dc22
                            2003016560

CONTENTS

Introduction   **6**

History of the Draft   10

POINT
An All-Volunteer Military Service
Endangers National Security   **22**

COUNTERPOINT
The United States Can Meet Its Military
Commitments Without a Draft   **36**

POINT
Reviving the Draft Would
Benefit Society   **48**

COUNTERPOINT
Reviving the Draft Would Do
More Harm Than Good   **60**

POINT
Even Without a Draft, a National Service
Requirement Would Benefit Society   **72**

COUNTERPOINT
A National Service Requirement is
Unnecessary and Unfair   **84**

The Future of Mandatory Service   96

Notes   **108**
Resources   **112**
Elements of the Argument   **114**
Appendix: Beginning Legal Research   **116**
Index   **120**

Introduction
Alan Marzilli, M.A., J.D.
Durham, North Carolina

The debates presented in POINT/COUNTERPOINT are among the most interesting and controversial in contemporary American society, but studying them is more than an academic activity. They affect every citizen; they are the issues that today's leaders debate and tomorrow's will decide. The reader may one day play a central role in resolving them.

Why study both sides of the debate? It's possible that the reader will not yet have formed any opinion at all on the subject of this volume—but this is unlikely. It is more likely that the reader will already hold an opinion, probably a strong one, and very probably one formed without full exposure to the arguments of the other side. It is rare to hear an argument presented in a balanced way, and it is easy to form an opinion on too little information; these books will help to fill in the informational gaps that can never be avoided. More important, though, is the practical function of the series: Skillful argumentation requires a thorough knowledge of *both* sides—though there are seldom only two, and only by knowing what an opponent is likely to assert can one form an articulate response.

Perhaps more important is that listening to the other side sometimes helps one to see an opponent's arguments in a more human way. For example, Sister Helen Prejean, one of the nation's most visible opponents of capital punishment, has been deeply affected by her interactions with the families of murder victims. Seeing the families' grief and pain, she understands much better why people support the death penalty, and she is able to carry out her advocacy with a greater sensitivity to the needs and beliefs of those who do not agree with her. Her relativism, in turn, lends credibility to her work. Dismissing the other side of the argument as totally without merit can be too easy—it is far more useful to understand the nature of the controversy and the reasons *why* the issue defies resolution.

The most controversial issues of all are often those that center on a constitutional right. The Bill of Rights—the first ten amendments to the U.S. Constitution—spells out some of the most fundamental rights that distinguish the governmental system of the United States from those that allow fewer (or other) freedoms. But the sparsely worded document is open to inter-pretation, and clauses of only a few words are often at the heart of national debates. The Bill of Rights was meant to protect individual liberties; but the needs of some individuals clash with those of society as a whole, and when this happens someone has to decide where to draw the line. Thus the Constitution becomes a battleground between the rights of individuals to do as they please and the responsibility of the government to protect its citizens. The First Amendment's guarantee of "freedom of speech," for example, leads to a number of difficult questions. Some forms of expression, such as burning an American flag, lead to public outrage—but nevertheless are said to be protected by the First Amendment. Other types of expression that most people find objectionable, such as sexually explicit material involving children, are not protected because they are considered harmful. The question is not only where to draw the line, but how to do this without infringing on the personal liberties on which the United States was built.

The Bill of Rights raises many other questions about indi-vidual rights and the societal "good." Is a prayer before a high school football game an "establishment of religion" prohibited by the First Amendment? Does the Second Amendment's promise of "the right to bear arms" include concealed handguns? Is stopping and frisking someone standing on a corner known to be frequented by drug dealers a form of "unreasonable search and seizure" in violation of the Fourth Amendment? Although the nine-member U.S. Supreme Court has the ultimate authority in interpreting the Constitution, its answers do not always satisfy the public. When a group of nine people—sometimes by a five-to-four vote—makes a decision that affects the lives of hundreds of millions, public outcry can be expected. And the composition of the Court does change over time, so even a landmark decision is not guaranteed to stand forever. The limits of constitutional protection are always in flux.

These issues make headlines, divide courts, and decide elections. They are the questions most worthy of national debate, and this series aims to cover them as thoroughly as possible. Each volume sets out some of the key arguments surrounding a particular issue, even some views that most people consider extreme or radical—but presents a balanced perspective on the issue. Excerpts from the relevant laws and judicial opinions and references to central concepts, source material, and advocacy groups help the reader to explore the issues even further and to read "the letter of the law" just as the legislatures and the courts have established it.

It may seem that some debates—such as those over capital punishment and abortion, debates with a strong moral component— will never be resolved. But American history offers numerous examples of controversies that once seemed insurmountable but now are effectively settled, even if only on the surface. Abolitionists met with widespread resistance to their efforts to end slavery, and the controversy over that issue threatened to cleave the nation in two; but today public debate over the merits of slavery would be unthinkable, though racial inequalities still plague the nation. Similarly unthinkable at one time was suffrage for women and minorities, but this is now a matter of course. Distributing information about contraception once was a crime. Societies change, and attitudes change, and new questions of social justice are raised constantly while the old ones fade into irrelevancy.

Whatever the root of the controversy, the books in POINT/ COUNTERPOINT seek to explain to the reader the origins of the debate, the current state of the law, and the arguments on both sides. The goal of the series is to inform the reader about the issues facing not only American politicians, but all of the nation's citizens, and to encourage the reader to become more actively involved in resolving these debates, as a voter, a concerned citizen, a journalist, an activist, or an elected official. Democracy is based on education, and every voice counts—so every opinion must be an informed one.

This volume explores the question of whether it is fair for the nation to require its young people to serve in the military or otherwise serve the country. The draft has been controversial since the Vietnam War, when thousands of young American men were drafted into the armed forces—and many of them killed—even as many citizens questioned whether the United States should be involved in Vietnam at all. The events of September 11, 2001, renewed calls for requiring young Americans to serve their country. However, the question remains as to who should serve: every young adult, every young man, or people chosen by a random lottery? This volume examines that central question, and also probes some of the different variants for military service. One option would be to allow the armed forces to draft people rather than relying on television recruiting ads. Another option, used in countries such as Israel and Switzerland, would be to require all young people to undergo military training, even if they do not serve in the armed forces. An alternative approach would be to require young people to serve their country in some capacity, including nonmilitary community service jobs. As the nation debates mandatory military service, the nation's youth wait to hear whether their lives will be drastically changed.

History of the Draft

The idea that members of a community have a duty to defend it is as old as civilization itself. In a free society like ours, forcing citizens to fight involves conflicting notions of civic duty, individual freedom, and equality. Although the United States has relied on an all-volunteer military for most of its history, it was forced to draft men to fight the Civil War and the wars of the twentieth century. Each of those drafts raised the fundamental question: Who serves when not all serve?

• **Do Americans take their freedom for granted?**

The Draft in Greece and Rome

The societies that gave the United States its political traditions expected every able-bodied man to render military service: "The idea that free men must be prepared to bear arms . . . derives from the Greek city-state that made it a condition of citizenship that all free men of property should purchase arms, train for war and do duty in time of danger." [1]

In Athens, a man turning 18 went into the army for two years. Afterward, he rejoined his fellow citizens but remained part of the reserves. City-states such as Athens provided the model for the "citizen-soldier."

Citizenship and military service also were linked in the Roman Republic. When an enemy threatened, citizens assembled on the Campus Martius, a field dedicated to the god of war. If they voted to fight, an army was chosen from among the eligible men. The Romans, like the Greeks, were citizens first, soldiers second. Legendary Roman General Cincinnatus was plowing his fields when messengers told him he had been given command of the army. After defeating the enemy, Cincinnatus went back to his farm, even turning down the honors that came with his victories.

The Colonial Militia Tradition

Citizen-soldiers, known as the *militia*, played an important role in England. The English colonists who settled America brought the idea of the militia with them. To protect settlements from Indian raids, most colonies required able-bodied men to attend regular drills and fight when needed. Militiamen fought with, and under the command of, their relatives and neighbors.

The colonial militia exempted men who were vital to civilian society, such as doctors and teachers. In addition, men whose religious beliefs forbade them to go to war were treated as "conscientious objectors" and allowed to serve in an alternate, noncombat role.

During the American Revolution, George Washington's Continental Army consisted of a small number of paid volunteers and a larger body of militiamen, some of whom were draftees. Americans of the time were aware of and accepted the idea of drafting men into the militia. For example, the Pennsylvania Constitution of 1776 provided "That every member of society hath a right to be protected in the enjoyment of life, liberty, and property, and therefore is bound to contribute his proportion toward the expense of that protection, and yield his personal service when necessary, or an equivalent thereto."[2]

After the war, the framers of the Constitution had a heated debate over how best to defend the country. Some insisted that war was becoming a science, and that "[i]rregular and untrained soldiers, no matter how courageous, could always be routed by a smaller but well-oiled machine of veterans."[3] But others were concerned that maintaining an army of paid professionals could lead to endless wars, or even a military dictatorship. The framers eventually compromised, giving Congress power "to raise and support Armies" and allowing the president to call up the militia "to execute the Laws of the Union, suppress Insurrections and repel Invasions."[4]

Warfare and the Draft in Nineteenth-Century America

George Washington was the first of a number of presidents to propose compulsory military training for all men: "[E]very *Citizen* who enjoys the protection of a free Government, owes not only a proportion of his property, but even of his personal services for the defense of it, and consequently that the *Citizens* of America . . . should be borne on the *Militia* rolls."[5]

Despite Washington's advice, the military remained an all-volunteer force. During the War of 1812, after the British burned the White House and the Capitol, President James Madison asked for authority to draft enough men to expel the invaders. Congress rejected the proposal, largely because of objections to putting the federal government in charge of the militia. The nation again relied on volunteers in the

Mexican War (1846–1848), but historians have criticized their performance.

At the start of the Civil War, both the Union and Confederacy called on men to enlist, and thousands did. It soon became clear that the war would be long and bloody, however, and that volunteers alone would not provide the needed manpower. In 1862, the Confederacy, which had a much smaller population, authorized a draft. A year later, Northern lawmakers followed suit. Despite a large pool of military-age men and the payment of bonuses as high as a thousand dollars—twice what the average man earned in a year—the military was not attracting enough volunteers to form an army strong enough to win the war.

Both the Union and Confederate draft laws allowed a man to hire a substitute to fight for him. Although the idea offends modern-day notions of justice, "The practice of allowing substitution was customary at that time, and was considered the most intelligent means of exempting men engaged in essential civilian occupations."[6] The law also allowed a man to avoid serving by paying a $300 "commutation fee" to the government.

- **What civilian jobs are so important that those who do them should not be drafted?**

Draftees and volunteers alike were given bonuses for serving. Historians contend the Union draft was not a true draft, but rather part of a "carrot-and-stick" approach to boost the number of volunteers. In fact, draftees accounted for only a tiny percentage of the men who served in the Union Army. Even so, many Northerners complained that the Civil War was "a rich man's war, a poor man's fight." Antidraft violence broke out in a number of cities. The worst unrest occurred in New York City, where antidraft protests degenerated into race riots; by some estimates, more than a thousand people, most of them African Americans, were killed.

(Continued on page 16)

The Draft in America: A Chronology

1607–1775   Most colonies require able-bodied men to bear arms, undergo military training, and fight when called on.

1775–1781   In the Revolutionary War, George Washington leads a force of paid enlistees and volunteer and draftee militiamen against the British.

1778   The Continental Congress urges the states to consider a draft. The idea is dropped when France enters the war on the American side.

1787   The framers send the Constitution to the states for ratification. It gives the states power over the militia and Congress the power to raise armies. It also authorizes the president to call up the militia in an emergency.

1792   Congress passes the Uniform Militia Act, which calls for the enrollment of men of military age. However, enforcement is left up to the states.

1814   The Madison administration asks Congress to authorize a draft, but lawmakers cannot agree on a law. After the War of 1812, the militia system goes into decline.

1846–1848   Relying on an all-volunteer force, the United States wins the Mexican War. However, the conflict lasts longer than expected.

1862   With far fewer military-age men than the Union, the Confederacy resorts to a draft to fill the army's manpower needs.

1863   The U.S. Congress authorizes a draft. Fewer than 3 percent of those who serve in the Union Army are draftees forced to serve in person.

1898   Congress passes a law that makes men subject to military duty. However, there is no national draft, and the Spanish-American War is fought with volunteers.

1917   Congress passes the Selective Service Act, the nation's first modern draft law. The following year, in the *Selective Draft Law Cases*, the Supreme Court finds the draft constitutional. A total of 2.8 million men — three out of four serving in the war — are draftees.

1940   In an effort to rebuild the military, Congress passes the Selective Training and Service Act. This act creates the nation's first peacetime draft.

1941–1945   After the United States enters World War II, Congress expands the draft. The class of draft-eligible men grows as the war continues. Ten million men are drafted.

1947   Congress allows the draft to expire and rejects the idea of universal military training.

1948	President Truman orders the armed forces to eliminate racial segregation. As the Cold War with the Soviet Union intensifies, Congress reinstates the draft. The draft is expanded in 1950 after the Korean War begins.
1951	Congress passes a new Universal Military Training and Service Act, which remains in effect until 1973.
1965	Escalating American involvement in the Vietnam War results in increased draft calls. Americans begin to criticize the fairness of the draft system.
1967	The Marshall Commission rejects calls to end the draft, but it urges reforms that would make the Selective Service System fairer.
1969	At President Nixon's request, Congress adopts two Marshall Commission recommendations: making 19-year-olds the group most vulnerable to the draft, and selecting men through a lottery based on birthdate.
1973	The United States ends its involvement in the Vietnam War. Congress allows the Selective Service Act to expire.
1974	President Gerald Ford offers clemency to draft-law violators and military deserters. Performing alternative civilian service is a condition of being pardoned.
1975	The Selective Service System places draft registration on "deep standby" status.
1977	President Jimmy Carter pardons most violators of the draft laws.
1980	Congress reactivates the requirement that men turning 18 register for the draft. The following year, in *Rotsker* v. *Goldberg*, the Supreme Court finds the male-only registration requirement constitutional.
1982	Congress passes the Solomon Amendment, which makes registering for the draft a condition of receiving federal student aid. Two years later, in *Selective Service* v. *Minnesota Public Interest Research Group*, the Supreme Court finds the law constitutional.
1990–1991	The United States mobilizes a force of regulars, National Guard troops, and reservists to defeat Iraq in Operation Desert Storm.
1992	A presidential commission recommends against drafting women. Two years later, the Defense Department takes the same position.
2003	Responding to calls to bring back the draft, the Defense Department reaffirms its support for an all-volunteer military.

(Continued from page 13)

After the Civil War, the United States again relied on a small volunteer army, backed up by the National Guard, which replaced the militia. However, warfare was changing rapidly, and the armed forces needed better-trained, better-equipped men than the National Guard could supply. After the Spanish-American War of 1898, some in the military concluded the armed forces were not prepared for a major conflict and called for a draft like that used in European countries.

Selective Service and the Modern Draft

When the United States entered World War I in 1917, Congress passed the Selective Service Act, which created a "modern" draft system. Every eligible man had to register; draftees were chosen by lottery; and draft boards, which decided who would serve, were staffed by civilians. The World War I draft established the principle of *selective service,* under which the military, which no longer needed every able-bodied man, drafted just enough soldiers to make up for a shortage of volunteers. Selective service also recognized that a nation had to mobilize its entire economy for war. Consequently, some men were considered more valuable in civilian roles—supporting a family, working in a weapons plant, or even staying in school—than in the military. Those men were given deferments, which excused them from serving as long as they contributed in some way to the war effort.

- **Is it fair that young men must bear the burden of defending their country?**

In 1940, after the Nazis swept across Europe, Congress authorized the nation's first peacetime draft. At first, the draft was relatively mild; draftees would serve only one year on active duty and they could not be sent overseas. After the Japanese attack on Pearl Harbor, though, Congress authorized the sending of draftees overseas, lowered the minimum draft age from 21 to 20, and required men to stay in the military for the duration of the war

It was during World War I (1914–1918) that the idea of selective service was first established in the United States. That war, which was the most devastating and most expensive ever fought to that time, showed the U.S. government that it was necessary to utilize the entire American population if it hoped to win a victory in the new style of warfare. Not only were men registered for the draft, but posters like this one also urged citizens to enlist as volunteers in the armed forces.

plus six additional months. As the war progressed, the class of men eligible for the draft grew larger; at one point, the military even considered drafting nurses when too few volunteered.

In an effort to prepare for future wars, President Harry Truman recommended that all men undergo military training. That proposal, however, died in Congress, which reinstated the World War II–style draft. Because of the Korean War and the Soviet threat, Congress kept the draft in place even though the nation was not officially at war. During the 1950s, the United States required a large military in case it went to war with the Soviet Union. As a result, most draft-age men served: college graduates, the sons of the rich, even celebrities such as Elvis Presley. Americans strongly supported the draft. In the 1960s, however, the Baby Boom generation reached military age, and the armed forces needed fewer men. As a result, draft calls diminished, and more and more men—especially students— were given deferments.

• **Would a draft prevent war or make it more likely?**

In 1965, however, the United States escalated its involvement in Vietnam. President Lyndon Johnson decided against calling up the reserves, fearing the political consequences of such a move. Instead, Johnson relied on the regular forces, which included a growing number of draftees—more than 300,000 a year at the height of the conflict. Americans grew frustrated with the war, and began to question whether the draft system was fair. Men from wealthy or influential families found ways to avoid going to Vietnam. Some received a series of deferments— student, then occupational, then fatherhood—and put off serving until they turned 35 and were too old to be taken. Others claimed conscientious-objector status; the complicated appeal process made it easier for those rich enough to afford a lawyer to stay out of combat. Those with connections—such as professional athletes and politicians' sons—enlisted in the National Guard or the reserves, which were kept home during the war. The end result was a perception that those sent to Vietnam were likely to be poor or members of minority groups.

- **Do the rich and well educated owe a bigger debt to their country than those who are less fortunate?**

Vietnam War protesters were not the only Americans who believed the draft was unfair. Some conservatives argued that

> [T]he draft was like a tax unfairly levied. It fell heaviest on those forced to serve, who were then paid poorly for their service. The rest, meanwhile, got national security at cut rates. This inequity could be removed only if the people paid the going rate for their military personnel, and that rate could be determined only if soldiers were recruited in the open market.[7]

The all-volunteer military gained political support. As a candidate for president, Richard Nixon promised to end the draft. After taking office, he appointed the Gates Commission, which recommended that the military become an all-volunteer force. Meanwhile, the Vietnam War wound down, and draft calls diminished. Congress allowed the draft to expire in 1973.

- **Is it moral for a person to evade the draft, even by perfectly legal means?**

After Vietnam, the Pentagon adopted the "Total Force" concept, under which the reserves would play a greater role in future conflicts: "The total force . . . made any deployment as large as Vietnam impossible unless the President took the political risk to call up the reserves. Such a step requires substantial justification accepted by the public whose lives would be disrupted by the call to arms."[8]

The all-volunteer military was almost a failure. During the 1970s, the armed services suffered from a shortage of qualified recruits and a high turnover rate, mainly because soldiers were still poorly paid compared to civilians. Critics demanded an end to the all-volunteer experiment. Calls to bring back the draft grew louder after the Soviet invasion of Afghanistan in 1979. President Jimmy Carter decided against reinstating the draft, but he did ask Congress to reactivate draft registration. Congress passed a law requiring men turning 18 to register, but it refused to extend that requirement to women. At the time, women were barred from most military assignments, and their presence in the armed forces was actually considered disruptive.

Under President Ronald Reagan, a supporter of the all-volunteer force, military pay and benefits improved. The performance and morale of the military improved dramatically, and support for the draft diminished. In 1991, Operation Desert Storm, which involved the biggest call-up of the reserves since the Korean War of 1950–1953, demonstrated the effectiveness of the all-volunteer military. ("Volunteer," in this case, refers to people who enlist to serve in the military of their own free will. They are paid for their services, so they are not volunteers in that sense.) After Desert Storm, a solid majority of Americans and most of Congress opposed bringing back the draft. However, some scholars and lawmakers continued to argue that America's interests were not served by relying on an army of professionals.

Supporters of the draft again grew more vocal after the September 11, 2001, terror attacks on the World Trade Center and the Pentagon and during the buildup leading to the 2003 war against Iraq. Nevertheless, the Pentagon reaffirmed its commitment to an all-volunteer military:

> Not only has the All-Volunteer Force proved to be cost efficient; it is also combat-effective. The AVF has established a hard-earned record of success: from winning the Cold War to restoring regional balance, to fighting non-state actors and being ready for an uncertain future. . . . Today, more than 30 years later, we find that the [Gates] Commission—and the Nation—got it right![9]

Currently, the U.S. military consists of some 1.4 million regulars, most of them serving three- and four-year commitments. There are also about 1.35 million members of the National Guard and Reserves, who generally serve six-year commitments that require spending one weekend a month plus two full weeks a year with their units.

- **Did the September 11 terror attacks change your opinion about going to war?**

Ancient democracies required all able-bodied men to defend their country; these men were citizens first and soldiers second. The framers of the Constitution preferred citizen-soldiers to a professional army, which it considered a threat to liberty. As warfare grew more sophisticated, though, it became impossible to rely on citizen-soldiers alone. The need for manpower forced the nation to draft men into the military. Modern drafts are based on the principle of selective service, in which not all eligible men are drafted. The American public generally supported the draft until Vietnam, when many believed it was too easy for the rich to avoid serving. The United States abolished the draft in 1973. Although the Pentagon and most civilian leaders oppose restoring it, some experts argue that relying on paid volunteers is unwise and dangerous.

An All-Volunteer Military Service Endangers National Security

I n this book, "the draft" refers to two related ideas: *conscription* and *universal military training.* Conscription means select- ing young men from the pool of those who are eligible and requiring those selected to serve for a given number of years or, in wartime, for the duration. America's twentieth-century drafts have followed the conscription model. Universal military training, on the other hand, means requiring all young men to undergo basic training, after which they return to civilian life but may be called up for service in case of war or national emergency. Switzerland has had universal military training for hundreds of years; Israel, surrounded by enemies, has it as well. The colonial militia came closest to an American version of universal military training. Whether they favor conscription, universal military training, or some combination of the two, supporters of the draft agree that it is too risky to rely on professional soldiers alone to defend our country.

- **Would conscription or universal military training make the United States a stronger nation?**

The Post–September 11 World Requires a Strong Military.

The September 11 terror attacks awakened the United States to threats from enemies both at home and abroad. President George W. Bush has told Americans repeatedly that their nation is at war against terrorists, and that the effort is worldwide and could last for many years. Experts believe the war on terror will not involve the clashes of massed armies depicted in movies such as *Saving Private Ryan*. Instead, it will be a series of low-level conflicts with terrorist cells, warring tribes, or drug cartels.

In an effort to break up terrorist organizations such as Al Qaeda, the United States has sent troops to a number of countries, including Afghanistan, Yemen, and the Philippines, to help local antiterror efforts. It will probably be necessary to continue sending American forces overseas. As President Bush explained: "To contend with uncertainty and to meet the many security challenges we face, the United States will require bases and stations within and beyond Western Europe and Northeast Asia, as well as temporary access arrangements for the long-distance deployment of U.S. forces."[10] Nor has the threat of conventional war disappeared—a reality made clear by the 2003 war against Iraq. The president has warned that the United States will strike first against "rogue states" that aid terrorism and possess weapons of mass destruction.

- **As the world's only superpower, does the United States have a responsibility to keep order overseas?**

(Continued on page 27)

Selective Draft Law Cases

At the time the Constitution was written, many of the framers believed the power to draft men belonged to the states, not the federal government. There were strong objections to President Madison's call for a draft during the War of 1812, and even fiercer opposition to the Civil War draft. Even so, the question of whether a national draft was constitutional did not reach the Supreme Court until World War I, when several men appealed their convictions for failing to report for induction.

In the *Selective Draft Law Cases*, 245 U.S. 366 (1918), the High Court unanimously held that the draft was constitutional. Speaking for the Court, Chief Justice Edward White first spelled out Congress's authority to draft men:

> [A]uthority to enact [the draft law] must be found in the clauses of the Constitution giving Congress power "to declare war . . . to raise and support armies . . . [and] to make rules for the government and regulation of the land and naval forces." And of course the powers conferred by these provisions like all other powers given carry with them as provided by the Constitution the authority "to make all laws which shall be necessary and proper for carrying into execution the foregoing powers. . . ."
>
> As the mind cannot conceive an army without the men to compose it, on the face of the Constitution the objection that it does not give power to provide for such men would seem to be too frivolous for further notice.

He swept aside the argument that the nation lacked power to require men to defend it:

> It may not be doubted that the very conception of a just government and its duty to the citizen includes the reciprocal obligation of the citizen to render military service in case of need, and the right to compel it.

The Chief Justice went on to explain that the draft has long been part of the Anglo-American tradition:

> In England it is certain that before the Norman Conquest the duty of the great militant body of the citizens was recognized and enforceable.

. . . It is unnecessary to follow the long controversy between Crown and Parliament as to the branch of the government in which the power resided, since there never was any doubt that it somewhere resided. . . .

In the Colonies before the separation from England there cannot be the slightest doubt that the right to enforce military service was unquestioned and that practical effect was given to the power in many cases. . . . In fact the duty of the citizen to render military service and the power to compel him against his consent to do so was expressly sanctioned by the Constitutions of at least nine of the states.

White then settled the long-standing controversy over whether Congress had to rely on the states to provide men for the armed forces:

When the Constitution came to be formed it may not be disputed that one of the recognized necessities for its adoption was the [lack] of power in Congress to raise an army and the dependence upon the states for their quotas. In supplying the power it was manifestly intended to give it all and leave none to the states.

Reviewing the history of the draft, he noted that the courts of six Confederate states had upheld a draft similar in principle to that being challenged.

Finally, the Chief Justice rejected a number of miscellaneous objections to the draft, including the argument that it amounted to involuntary servitude:

[W]e are unable to conceive upon what theory the exaction by government from the citizen of the performance of his supreme and noble duty of contributing to the defense of the rights and honor of the nation as the result of a war declared by the great representative body of the people can be said to be the imposition of involuntary servitude in violation of the prohibitions of the Thirteenth Amendment.

The 2003 war in Iraq was an example of how effective the all-volunteer U.S. military can be. These marines from the 2nd Battalion, 1st Marine Regiment are seen escorting captured enemy prisoners to a holding area. Despite this enormous success, though, many people argue that as Americans continue to take on peacekeeping missions and other military responsibilities overseas, the traditional volunteer force will no longer be enough. In fact, some critics claim that the current deployment of troops is already so widespread that homeland-security interests are being compromised, making the nation more vulnerable to terrorist and other attacks.

(Continued from page 23)

- **Which is a more serious threat: terrorists or a dictator with nuclear weapons?**

Whether or not this country fights another conventional war, our military will be heavily involved overseas. In the post–Cold War world, weak countries actually represent a more serious threat than strong ones. "Failing states," with weak central governments and porous borders, can become havens for terrorists. Afghanistan under the Taliban was such a state, and there are others in Asia and Africa. To reestablish the rule of law in these countries, the United States may send forces to keep the peace until a new government is put in place and order restored. Some experts consider "nation building" and peacekeeping missions well suited to draftees. According to Professor Charles Moskos, a longtime supporter of the draft: "Military police work doesn't require that many special skills. . . . Short-term draftees, in other words, could easily do these M.P. jobs, and many others besides. This would free up more professional soldiers to fight the war on terrorism without requiring the U.S. to abandon other commitments."[11]

The war against terror also has had a serious impact at home. Political columnist David Broder warns that homeland defense could be as labor-intensive as the major conflicts of the last century. States and cities, already facing financial problems, have been hurt by the call-up of reserve units to join the fighting in Afghanistan and Iraq. The call-up has cost them skilled personnel, especially health-care workers, firefighters, and law-enforcement officers. In addition, homeland-security responsibilities have created a need for trained personnel in a variety of capacities, including guarding power plants and dams, handling border and airport security, and responding to emergencies. Some believe draftees can be trained to perform many of these tasks.

The Military Cannot Meet Its Needs With Volunteers.

After Vietnam, the United States substantially reduced the size of the military; today, there are about 1.4 million personnel on active duty, compared to about 3.5 million during the 1960s. Critics of the all-volunteer force believe that this country has scaled back its military too much. Even before the war on terror began, supporters of the draft argued that the armed forces were having trouble attracting enough skilled men and women. They warned that it would be impossible to find enough volunteers should the world situation make another military buildup necessary.

- **Should the government be asking citizens to make greater sacrifices in the war against terror?**

Even though the armed forces continue to meet their recruiting goals, some maintain they have done so by resorting to "quick fixes" that will have a serious long-term impact. The military pay raises that attracted recruits have added tens of billions of dollars to the defense budget. Even after those raises, military salaries are still not on par with salaries for comparable civilian jobs. By one estimate, it would take an additional $30 billion a year to close the pay gap.

Critics of the all-volunteer military argue that bonuses paid to new recruits—as much as $20,000 for those who sign up for a combat assignment—have hurt the morale of career soldiers, who are the most valuable members of the armed forces. They claim that financial incentives to join have created a force of "overpaid recruits and underpaid sergeants" and caused an exodus of pilots, technicians, and sailors frustrated over low pay and lack of respect. Supporters believe that a draft would allow the military to cut recruits' pay and use the money to give career soldiers a badly needed raise.

During the all-volunteer era, the percentage of married enlisted personnel has risen to nearly 50 percent. Many married service members, and some single ones as well, care for children. The result has been time constraints and financial problems that sometimes have proved disruptive. Most draft-age men, on the other hand, have not yet started families.

- **Should single parents be allowed to serve in the military?**

One of the most controversial strategies for filling the ranks has been opening most jobs to women, who today account for 15 percent of the military. Critics complain that the Pentagon has watered down job requirements, especially those relating to physical strength, in order to accommodate women. According to the Hoover Institution's Stanley Kurtz, if the military went back to its traditional standards, so few women would qualify that a draft would become necessary. Some also contend that efforts to get women to enlist have made the armed forces less attractive to men. They note that while the number of female recruits has increased, male enlistments have fallen off. This trend concerns Eagle Forum founder Phyllis Schlafly, who states:

> The purpose of the military is to defend Americans against the bad guys of the world. The warrior culture, with tough, all-male training, is what attracts young men into the armed services and motivates them to sacrifice personal comfort and safety while serving their country in uniform. . . . It's no wonder that the services can't fill their recruitment goals for a feminized military.[12]

- **Has the military weakened itself by encouraging women to join?**

Critics of the free-market approach warn that financial incentives to volunteer threaten the military's unique culture. Many who have spent their lives in uniform are proud to belong to an institution that is different and that has resisted the self-centeredness and lack of discipline of civilian life. Some worry that efforts to "market" the armed forces—such as the much-criticized "An Army of One" campaign—will turn military service into "just another job" and set back recruiting for years to come. Even the Gates Commission conceded that problems might result from "civilianization," which could break down the armed services' unique culture and make those in the military less effective in battle.

The Selective Service System's Lewis B. Hershey

Lewis B. Hershey was born in Angola, Indiana, in 1893. The son of middle-class parents, he lived on a farm and became a teacher after finishing high school. To make extra money, Hershey joined the Indiana National Guard. It was the beginning of a distinguished military career during which he rose to the rank of four-star general.

In 1916, as a young second lieutenant, Hershey was part of a force sent to the Mexican border to fight rebel General Pancho Villa. He got a firsthand look at how unprepared the United States was for war, and he became convinced of the need for universal military training.

During the 1930s, as Germany prepared for war, Hershey and other officers were assigned to set up a mechanism that would oversee a possible draft. Soon after Congress reinstated the draft and created the Selective Service System, Hershey became its director.

Even though he wore a military uniform, Hershey was a supporter of civilian control over the Selective Service. He believed decisions about whether to draft someone were best left to his neighbors, who were most familiar with individual circumstances. He also kept the system simple enough for the average American to understand. His approach was a success. Selective Service provided the manpower needed to win World War II, and the public believed that the draft was run fairly. Hershey was popular and respected despite the fact that he headed the agency that took men away from their families and sent them into war. His country wit made him an ideal spokesman for the Selective Service, and his ability to get along with Congress earned political support for both himself and the draft.

For Hershey, the postwar years were more difficult than the war itself. The

- **Do recruiting ads cheapen the image of the armed forces? Are they believable?**

Finally, there is the lingering question of the all-volunteer military's readiness. Since the end of the Vietnam War, the United States has not been involved in a bloody, drawn-out conflict. As result, there are fears that Americans might not be

military needed fewer men, forcing Hershey—who still believed that every man should serve—to agree to more and more deferments. Selective Service became a mechanism for "channeling" men into useful occupations, and the draft was a means of prodding them to enlist.

The 1960s proved to be Hershey's downfall. A product of small-town America, he never wavered from his belief in duty, patriotism, and traditional values. In Hershey's view, a stint in the military made men healthier; and wars, which were as inevitable as natural disasters, focused the nation on the greater good. Hershey also believed that a woman's place was in the home. As a young man, he had opposed giving women the right to vote; as head of the Selective Service, he was against putting women on draft boards. When students protested the Vietnam War, Hershey angrily denounced college professors and the news media for encouraging antiwar activity. When protesters occupied Selective Service offices, he urged draft boards to move them to the top of the list for induction.

By the time President Nixon took office, Hershey was a political liability. As historian George Flynn put it, "As an old man with the job of drafting young men, he symbolized to many the failure of the establishment." In October 1969, Nixon, who opposed the draft, "reassigned" Hershey to a presidential advisor position with no real authority.

Hershey headed the Selective Service System for 33 years, serving under six different presidents. Under his direction, more than 14.5 million men were inducted into the armed forces. A good soldier until the end, Hershey's last major duty was to organize the draft lottery—an idea he had firmly opposed for years.

Source: George Q. Flynn, *Lewis B. Hershey, Mr. Selective Service*. Chapel Hill: University of North Carolina Press, 1985.

willing to accept the casualties such a conflict would bring. They point, for example, to President Bill Clinton's decision to pull American troops out of Somalia after a series of attacks by local warlords. Charles Moskos blames the nation's lack of resolve on our all-volunteer military: "Only when the upper classes perform military service has the public at large defined the cause to be worth young people's lives. Only when privileged youth are on the firing line do war losses become more acceptable. Citizens accept hardships only when their leadership is viewed as self-sacrificing."[13]

Civilians and the Military Are Too Isolated From One Another.

Although the United States has the world's strongest military, a large peacetime army is not part of our tradition. The framers of the Constitution were leery of a force of paid professionals. They had reason to be suspicious. During early colonial days, England was torn by a running battle between the king and Parliament. One issue in that struggle was the king's paid army, which many Englishmen accused of oppressing the people. The framers' concerns about standing armies are still relevant. Former Senator Gary Hart warned: "Political and military leaders will be powerfully tempted to play Great Power games, using standing armies as chess pieces in the never-ending struggle for hegemony, influence, and prestige."[14] Supporters of the citizen-soldier tradition believe the draft is needed to stop military commanders from starting foolish wars. General John McAuley Palmer argued, "Only if the entire military were stocked with civilians, from raw recruits to high-ranking officers, could the nation be protected against adventurism and other abuse of military power."[15]

- **Was it a mistake to downsize the military so drastically after the draft ended?**

Because there is no draft, the percentage of Americans who have served in the military is shrinking. The result is a growing sense of isolation; many civilians are ignorant of military life, and some in the military are disgusted with civilian society. Senator John McCain, who spent six years as a prisoner of war in North Vietnam, warns: "We should also be concerned by the growing gap between our nation's military and civilian cultures. While the volunteer military has been successful, fewer Americans know and appreciate the sacrifices and contributions of their fellow citizens who serve in uniform." [16]

Fewer enlistments have meant fewer veterans among our political leaders. During the Vietnam War, three out of four members of Congress had served in the military; today, that proportion has fallen to one in three. The dwindling number of veterans concerns lawmakers like McCain: "In the past, it has been a rite of passage for our nation's leaders to serve in the armed forces. Today, fewer and fewer of my congressional colleagues know from experience the realities of military life. The decline of the citizen-soldier is not healthy for a democracy." [17]

Our lawmakers' isolation from the military is one reason why Representative Charles Rangel, a Korean War veteran, sponsored a bill that would reinstate the draft. Rangel explained: "[T]he Congress that voted overwhelmingly in favor to allow the use of force in Iraq includes only one member who has a child in the enlisted ranks of the military—just a few more have children who are officers." [18]

Some advocates of the draft argue that lawmakers who never served in the military are ignorant of or uninterested in defense issues, and that the result has been a bloated defense budget and a military establishment that resists civilians' efforts to reform it.

- **Is a lawmaker with military experience more likely to support going to war? Or vice versa?**

Our leaders' lack of military experience has even made the public cynical about their decisions relating to war. Public officials who took advantage of deferments to avoid military service, but now favor hard-line policies have been labeled "chicken hawks." Conversely, President Clinton's widely publicized efforts to avoid the draft after finishing college became an issue in his presidential campaign. Even after Clinton was elected, there was widespread resentment over the idea of having a commander-in-chief who had been so hostile toward the military.

> • **How important is it to have a president who has served in the military?**

Finally, many believe that Americans have become dangerously apathetic toward their country's foreign policy. Combat veteran and military correspondent David Hackworth argues that a draft would force Americans to think about developments oversears. He offers Vietnam as an example:

> [W]hile almost everyone deployed to 'Nam instantly knew it was a bad war and that our forces were ill-trained to fight their veteran guerrilla opponent, no one sounded off. Not until the draft kicked in and planeloads of dead conscripts began coming home in caskets did America's moms and dads start asking hard questions and getting the straight skinny from their sons.[19]

Hackworth believes that draftees provide a form of checks and balances on the military. Unlike career soldiers trained to obey orders, draftees are willing to "blow the whistle" on waste and corruption.

The United States is engaged in a global war against terrorists and the states that sponsor them. The war, which may last for years, will demand a stepped-up effort by our military, both overseas and at home. For years, the armed forces have struggled to meet recruiting goals, and it may be difficult to find enough volunteers for another military buildup. Relying on higher pay and more benefits to encourage enlistments has weakened the military. Thirty years without a draft have isolated Americans from military life and created public apathy toward foreign policy. In addition, our leaders' lack of military experience may lead to unwise decisions about going to war.

The United States Can Meet Its Military Commitments Without a Draft

The invention of more advanced—and deadly—weapons has meant constant changes in the way wars are fought. The Industrial Revolution made it possible to mass-produce weapons, while the combination of cheap arms and a military draft enabled nations to send huge armies into battle. Both world wars involved tens of millions of soldiers, along with the mobilization of entire economies for war. By contrast, modern wars are won with satellites, computers, wireless communications, and "smart" weapons that can be fired at targets hundreds or even thousands of miles away. Technical sophistication, not manpower, is the key to victory.

Modern Warfare Requires Fewer but Better-Trained Soldiers.

The nature of warfare has changed dramatically since the United States mobilized more than 16 million troops to fight the Axis powers in World War II. The successful campaign to topple Afghanistan's Taliban government after the September 11 terror attacks gave Americans a glimpse of how future wars will be fought. As the Cato Institute's Doug Bandow observed:

> Technical skills will become even more important in the future, especially since anti-terrorism has surpassed conventional defense as America's most important security goal. Masses of cannon fodder are of dubious value even in a typical conventional war today, given the killing potential of well-trained soldiers using the latest technology. . . .
>
> The value of special forces was obvious enough in the attack on the Taliban government . . . Action in Somalia or elsewhere would require a similar, well-targeted approach, not a huge occupying army.[20]

- **Do television shows and movies realistically portray war? Do they tend to glorify it?**

Having been downsized since Vietnam and ordered to rely on volunteers, the armed forces have learned to make do with fewer soldiers. According to the Defense Department: "The high-aptitude, high-experience [all-volunteer military] has encouraged the Department to leverage its weapons procurement in the direction of systems that are equally or more lethal, while requiring fewer (albeit smarter and more experienced) people."[21] Put simply, today's military is not compatible with a force made up of draftees.

During the early years of the all-volunteer force, skeptics—including many in the military—warned that it would be impossible to attract enough qualified personnel. Defense Secretary Donald Rumsfeld, however, believes that the doubters have been proven wrong:

> Now, are we able today to maintain a force that is at the appropriate size by paying people roughly what they'd be

making in the civilian manpower market? Yes. Are we doing it today? Yes. Are we meeting the recruiting goals? Yes. Have we been able to attract and retain people in the Guard and the Reserves who can augment that force when necessary, such as today? Yes, we have.[22]

Though the armed forces sometimes have struggled to meet their recruiting goals, those problems have been temporary. For example, two of the worst years for recruiting were 1998 and 1999. However, that was a time when the economy was booming and young Americans found it easy to find high-paying jobs. By 2001, all of the military services had met their recruiting goals; furthermore, the overwhelming majority of enlistees had high school diplomas and scored above average on military aptitude tests.

> • **Is a career in the military more honorable than one in law enforcement or firefighting?**

A Draft Would Impair the Military's Effectiveness.

The shift to an all-volunteer force has forced military commanders to treat soldiers as valuable resources rather than as cheap, easily replaceable equipment. Consequently, the manpower provided by a draft would be better suited to fight wars of the past than those to come. Johns Hopkins Professor Eliot Cohen remarked, "Conscripts are good if you're fighting your next-door neighbor. They're not nearly so effective for the peacekeeping and long-distance military operations that are much more likely for today's military forces."[23] Bringing back the draft might discourage the military from buying weapons designed for highly trained soldiers and force it to rely instead on labor-intensive equipment that would create the need for even more draftees. If recruits are paid below-market wages, as they were during the draft era, the armed forces might also be tempted to take in more troops than needed. The result would be the accumulation of excess forces. The practice

FROM THE BENCH

Holmes v. *United States*: Is a Peacetime Draft Constitutional?

The last declared war fought by the United States was World War II. All the fighting that followed, including the Vietnam War and both wars against Iraq, took place without a formal declaration. Some people have raised the issue of whether the country was in fact "at war" during these conflicts.

In 1967, Albert Holmes, a Jehovah's Witness minister and a conscientious objector to the Vietnam War, was convicted of refusing to report for alternate civilian work. Holmes appealed his conviction, arguing that drafting men in peacetime was a form of involuntary servitude prohibited by the Constitution.

A federal appeals court denied Holmes's appeal, ruling that Congress's power to draft men was not limited to times of declared war or national emergency. In *Holmes* v. *United States*, 391 U.S. 396 (1968), the Supreme Court refused to review the appeals court's decision. However, Justice William Douglas wrote a dissenting opinion in which he argued that a serious question existed as to whether Congress had the power to draft during peacetime. Turning to the conflict in Vietnam, he observed:

> Putting down an internal insurrection, like defending our shores against an aggressor, is certainly quite different from launching hostilities against a nation or a people overseas. I express no opinion on the merits. But there is a weighty view that what has transpired respecting Vietnam is unconstitutional, absent a declaration of war; that the Tonkin Gulf Resolution is no constitutional substitute for a declaration of war; that the making of appropriations was not an adequate substitute; and that "executive war-making is illegal."

Justice Douglas emphasized the importance of deciding, once and for all, the constitutionality of a peacetime draft:

> It is an important question. It is a recurring question. It is coming to us in various forms in many cases as a result of the conflict in Vietnam. I think we owe to those who are being marched off to jail for maintaining that a declaration of war is essential for conscription an answer to this important undecided constitutional question.

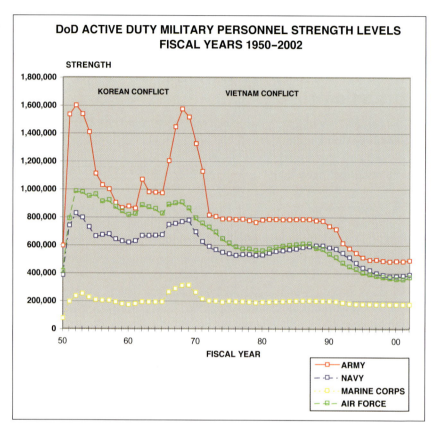

DoD ACTIVE DUTY MILITARY PERSONNEL STRENGTH LEVELS FISCAL YEARS 1950–2002

Over the years, depending on whether the nation was at war and whether there was a draft in effect or not, the armed forces have been at extremely different levels of strength. During the Korean and Vietnam wars, for instance, the number of Americans serving in the army alone reached as high as 1.6 million, whereas during the late 1990s, all branches of the military had fewer than 600,000 members each. This Department of Defense chart shows the varying levels of personnel strength in the U.S. military from 1950 through 2002.

of underpaying draftees also tends to perpetuate the draft: Low pay reduces the number of volunteers, which, in turn, leads to higher draft calls. In any event, the draft is not an effective way of finding the kind of manpower that today's military needs. Doug Bandow explains: "A draft is unable to provide a long-term supply of any skill: absent lifetime conscription, most draftees will leave when their tour [of duty] ends. And a draft cannot quickly fill an unexpected need."[24] As a result, some experts advise the military to rely on specialized reserve units, or even private contractors, to provide individuals with hard-to-find talents.

- **Would you support a draft for people with special skills, such as being fluent in a foreign language?**

Another consequence of the draft would be higher turnover. As the Defense Department points out: "During the most recent draft, 90 percent of conscripts quit after their initial two-year hitch, whereas retention of volunteers is five times better—about half remain after their initial (normally four-year) military service obligation."[25] Turnover would seriously hamper the armed forces because they need experienced, well-trained fighters to win modern wars. It would also be costly. Any savings resulting from low pay for draftees would be canceled out by the increased costs of training replacements for those who leave after two years.

Finally, a draft would make the armed forces harder to manage. Draftees would be less motivated than volunteers. As a senior Defense Department official explained:

> Instead of [draftees] being there in a class where the instructor's main objective is to keep everyone awake, now you have young people [volunteers] who are intent on learning their craft. They are professionals. They want to know how to do this, they want to know how to do it well, because they want to get ahead. They want to be promoted.[26]

A draft would also create discipline problems. One reason why the armed forces prefer volunteers is that they have chosen to accept the military's culture of obedience and selflessness. According to the Pentagon, fewer soldiers today are punished for serious offenses, such as using drugs or being absent without leave, than was the case during the draft era. It is believed that volunteers behave better because they want to avoid being discharged for breaking the rules. With an all-volunteer force, the armed services have the luxury of "firing" poor performers. Currently, they discharge about a third of their recruits early, most often for physical deficiencies or for failing to meet performance standards. If the draft is brought back, however, the armed services "can ill afford to kick out even the

Making the Draft Fairer: The Marshall Commission Report

Faced with growing criticism of the draft, President Johnson created a commission to examine the Selective Service System and recommend ways of reforming it. The so-called Marshall Commission examined proposals ranging from universal military training to an all-volunteer force.

The commission rejected alternatives to the existing selective draft. It concluded that an all-volunteer military was not flexible enough to provide large numbers of men in future crises. It found no need for universal military training. It also concluded that mandatory national service raised difficult issues, including whether such a program would even be constitutional.

However, the commission believed that the current system needed reform. Its major recommendations included the following:

- The Selective Service System should adopt consistent nationwide policies for giving deferments and exemptions, and it should inform men of their right to appeal draft board decisions.

- Draft boards should represent all elements of the public, and women should be allowed to serve on them.

- The current system, in which the oldest men were drafted first, should be replaced with a system making age 19 the year of greatest vulnerability. Draftees should be chosen by lottery. Men not taken at the end of the year should not be drafted later, except in an emergency.

worst malcontent since being kicked out would be seen as a reward for anyone seeking an out."[27]

> • **Have Americans become too undisciplined? Would universal military training reverse that trend?**

There Are Alternatives to a Draft.

Thirty years of experience have shown that incentives can attract enough qualified recruits to make a draft unnecessary. Despite

- Men should be given physical and mental examinations as soon as possible after turning 18, and those rejected should be given help that would enable them to meet the military's standards.

- Student and occupational deferments should be phased out. Those already in college would keep their deferments until they earned their bachelor's degree. Those not yet in college would, if called, be deferred only until the end of their sophomore year.

- Hardship deferments should still be granted.

- The current test for conscientious-objector status — being opposed to war in general — should stay in force.

- The need for draftees should be reduced by increasing opportunities for women to serve, and by offering remedial training to volunteers rejected by the military.

- Men who have been classified I-A (immediately eligible for military service) should not be allowed to enlist in the National Guard or the reserves to avoid being drafted.

Source: National Advisory Commission on Selective Service, *In Pursuit of Equity: Who Serves When Not All Serve? Report of the National Advisory Commission on Selective Service.* Washington, D.C.: U.S. Government Printing Office, 1967.

problems during the early years, and again during the late 1990s, the all-volunteer military is considered the best force in American history.

Military pay has improved greatly since the draft era, but remains about 15 percent below comparable civilian pay. If a deteriorating world situation forces the United States to beef up its military, or another economic boom gives young people less of an incentive to enlist, another pay raise could make the services more attractive.

Benefits other than salary also could boost enlistments, though. A new version of the GI Bill might appeal to college-bound individuals who currently would not consider entering the military. In 1998, a panel created by Congress recommended giving four years of tuition, plus $400 a month, to those who completed a four-year enlistment. Although such a generous benefit would be expensive, it would be money well spent; society would ultimately benefit from tens of thousands of educated, productive veterans entering the economy.

Improved retirement benefits, even for those who do not make a career of the military, might also attract recruits. It has been suggested that a retirement plan similar to a civilian 401(k) account "could be a powerful recruiting tool if structured to meet the desires of a twenty-first-century worker, especially if it includes things like personal choice, competitive returns on investment, transferability, and vesting short of 20 years." [28]

• **If you were in charge of recruiting, how would you "sell" military service to young people?**

There are also nonfinancial ways to encourage enlistments. One is a more effective recruiting campaign stressing benefits that cannot be measured in dollars and cents: travel, adventure, and the chance to learn new skills, for example. Some recommend "selling" the challenge of military life. Observers note that the Marine Corps, despite its reputation for tough discipline and rigorous physical standards, consistently meets its recruiting goals.

Other possibilities include offering a short-term enlistment program and allowing enlisted personnel more flexibility in leaving the service after their initial commitment. If recruiting problems become persistent, the services can simply lower their current standards and offer remedial education and training. As it is, they lose thousands of recruits they would have accepted during the draft era.

Finally, the rest of society could play a part in encouraging Americans to serve. As Doug Bandow observes, "Just as voters in some states look to community service—such as time spent in the volunteer fire department—as a criterion for election to office, so could voters consider service in the military."[29]

- **Would you be more likely to vote for a candidate who once served in the military?**

The All-Volunteer Military Has Succeeded on the Battlefield.

At the end of the Vietnam War, public support for the draft had fallen off, the armed services suffered from low morale and discipline problems, and some experts even worried whether the United States and its allies could defend Europe against a Soviet invasion. Something had to be done. Reformers saw the military's problems as an opportunity to carry out a bold experiment: a force composed entirely of volunteers. However, even the Gates Commission questioned how well that force would perform in a war.

That question was answered in 1991, when President George H.W. Bush sent an all-volunteer force to fight in Operation Desert Storm. That force ended Iraq's occupation of Kuwait and inflicted heavy casualties on the Iraqi Army, which, at the time, was one of the world's largest. Victory in Desert Storm earned the military strong popular support and gave it the image of a winning organization—one that people wanted to be part of. The victory was a political one as well. As military analyst James Burk observed: "The Reserve Component contribution serves to keep close bonds between the military and the civilian community. These reservists/guardsmen are construction workers, teachers, coaches, firemen, policemen, nurses, doctors, and lawyers in communities all across the nation."[30]

> • **Are volunteers more aggressive than draftees? Is an all-volunteer force more likely to start wars?**

Those reservists who left their families and careers to go to war had more political influence in their communities than did 19-year-old draftees. As a result, President Bush, unlike Presidents Johnson and Nixon, had to win the war quickly with minimal casualties. Burk also believes that Desert Storm showed that the citizen-soldier tradition was alive and well:

> After the event, there was debate about the readiness of some reserve units—especially those designated as combat units. But there was no debate about whether the reserve call-up helped forge political support for waging the conflict. Reconfiguring the military in this way emphasized the responsibilities of citizens for national defense. In effect, it revived the traditional republican belief that the state must have the consent of the citizens before marching to war.[31]

Finally, the concept of an all-volunteer military has taken root around the world. According to a senior Defense Department official, the American military has become "the envy of the world." Civilian and military leaders elsewhere have come to realize that a well-trained volunteer force is a more effective way of staffing the armed forces. A number of European Union countries have either abolished the draft recently or are planning to do so. Even Russia and China have made their military less labor-intensive and more technically sophisticated.

- **Is the "citizen-soldier" ideal still alive? Or has it become a myth?**

Modern warfare, in which highly skilled soldiers operate sophisticated weapons, requires fewer but better-trained personnel than wars of the past did. The draft is no longer an efficient way to find the qualified people the armed forces need. Draftees often leave before they can be taught important skills, and they also create motivation and disciplinary problems while in service. Improved pay and benefits, and greater respect for those serving, have encouraged enough enlistments and reenlistments to make a draft unnecessary. Despite fears that ending the draft would attract the unskilled and uneducated, the all-volunteer military is considered the best-qualified force in the nation's history.

Reviving the Draft Would Benefit Society

The decision to end the draft was based largely on an economic theory that considered military service a tax and the armed forces an industry that had to compete for workers. However, critics of the free-market approach consider it contrary to the American tradition of civic responsibility. They believe that a recruiting strategy that emphasizes financial rewards is a modern form of commutation, a practice that allowed men from well-to-do families to buy their way out of the military. Critics also fear that the all-volunteer military has created a generation of Americans who have forgotten that they owe a duty to their country and who have become unconcerned about their fellow citizens.

- **Do young people today love their country as much as their parents and grandparents do?**

The All-Volunteer Military Does Not Represent America.

It is a basic American belief that every citizen should be treated equally, regardless of race or social status. Although ours is a capitalist society, we believe that there are places where money has no place; for example, it is illegal to sell body parts or to offer one's vote to the highest bidder. Many think wealth should not decide who serves their country, and that the draft is an effective way of making sure that duty is shared by all segments of society.

Today's military no longer represents the society it defends. A *New York Times* reporter has described its enlisted ranks as "a mirror of working-class America." Though high entry standards have kept out the "underclass"—that is, those with little education and not much hope of finding a job— there are few men and women from wealthy families in the military. Many middle- and upper-class parents discourage their children from enlisting, either because there are better opportunities in civilian life or because they consider the armed forces "not good enough." College-bound Americans are most likely to avoid the military. In 1956, two-thirds of Professor Charles Moskos's Princeton graduating class had served, compared to less than 2 percent of Princeton's class of 1999. The same is true at other universities; as a result, only a small percentage of enlisted personnel have college degrees. Moskos believes this hurts the military because smarter soldiers make better fighters: "Research evidence serves to confirm the observation of commanders and [noncommissioned officers] who remember the draft period: the presence of middle-class, upwardly mobile men immeasurably boosts the morale of military units in peacetime as well as in war."[32]

- **How can the military get more college graduates to enlist? Can it do so without a draft?**

Although Americans no longer have to join the military, economic circumstances leave many with no alternative but to enlist:

> Direct economic incentives such as pay, cash bonuses, loan repayment programs and college money appeal most to those who [have] the greatest economic disadvantages. That is, those incentives have greatest appeal to those with the fewest alternatives in the college or labor market relative to their peers. . . . Continuing with business as usual will lead to an "economic conscription."[33]

People with few opportunities in civilian life are more likely to enlist in the military and stay there. The result is a force with a heavy representation of working-class Americans, including rural whites and, especially, African Americans. The high percentage of African Americans (who make up 20 percent of enlisted men and 32 percent of enlisted women, compared to their being only 12 percent of the population as a whole) is as much the product of discrimination and unequal distribution of wealth as the military's color-blind policies. Were it not for a high rejection rate, the percentage of African-American soldiers would be higher still.

Some political leaders are concerned that the duty of defending the country is not shared equally the way it was during the draft era. According to the Democratic Leadership Council:

> No obligation is more fundamental to citizenship than that of preserving our free institutions. While all wage-earning citizens contribute to the common defense by paying taxes, only a fraction assume the personal risk and sacrifice of military service. . . .
>
> In a democracy, however, citizenship requires not just sharing burdens, but sharing them equally. That is why Americans should be concerned that our armed forces today are not representative of society as a whole.[34]

An unrepresentative military could have dire consequences. Some worry about the rise of a "warrior caste," "often perpetuating itself from father to uncle to son or niece, whose political and cultural attitudes do not reflect the diversity found in civilian society—potentially foreshadowing a social schism between those who fight and those who ask them to."[35] There is also evidence that the officer corps is more politically conservative than the population as a whole—a trend that might strain relations between the military and its civilian commanders. Supporters of the draft are also concerned that the Pentagon's dollars-and-cents approach will do lasting damage to the ideals of duty and service to country. The late historian and author Stephen Ambrose raised the possibility that the military could become filled with impoverished soldiers with no connection to the rest of society—a force much like the British Army that lost the Revolutionary War. Charles Moskos is even more blunt: "If we are truly going to have armed forces based on cost-effective grounds—ignoring moral sentiments and civic dimensions— then we should simply hire Third World nationals to man our military and be done with it."[36] Some foresee even more serious consequences. The Democratic Leadership Council warns: "More than simple fairness is at stake. We must also ask ourselves: how long can a democratic republic survive if its most fortunate and capable citizens—America's future leaders—feel little obligation to contribute to its defense and well-being?"[37]

• **Do Americans look down on men and women in the military?**

Reviving the Draft Would Strengthen Democratic Values.

While the military has been criticized for being too conservative, and often justifiably so, it also has been a force for positive social change. During World War II, the African-American Tuskegee Airmen and the Japanese Americans of the 442nd Regimental Combat Team served with distinction, helping to eliminate

Many critics of the draft argue that the Selective Service tended to force more African Americans and other minorities into military service than whites and, especially, the rich. Interestingly, prior to the 1940s, the military was segregated, and black soldiers were not allowed to fight alongside whites. Attitudes toward black soldiers changed during World War II, when the Tuskegee Airmen (members of which are seen here in September 1942 with their instructor, Second Lieutenant Gabe C. Hawkins) became the first black combat unit in the U.S. Army Air Corps.

stereotypes about the loyalty and fighting ability of members of minority groups. Years before the Supreme Court ordered an end to segregated schools and Congress banned discrimination in restaurants, in the workplace, and at the polls, President Truman ordered the military to integrate. During the 1950s and 1960s, troops enforced court orders opening all-white schools to African-American students. More recently, the armed forces have been deployed to stop the flow of illegal drugs across our borders.

Even though our nation has become increasingly diverse, Americans tend to avoid people who are different from themselves. Even the public schools, the only experience most Americans have in common, are losing their influence as more families send their children to private schools or educate them at home. Some maintain that the military, which has traditionally served as a unique melting pot, is the right institution to bring Americans back together. Stephen Ambrose pointed out that during World War II and the Cold War,

> Americans from every group got together in the service, having a common goal—to defend their country—and, of course, a common experience. They learned together, pledged allegiance together, sweated together, hated their drill sergeants together, got drunk together, went overseas together. What they had in common—patriotism, a language, a past they could emphasize and venerate—mattered far more than what divided them.[38]

- **Is the country too divided by racial and religious differences? Would a draft heal those differences?**

An argument often made for universal military training is that it is democratic. Political commentator William F. Buckley points out that Switzerland, a country with several official languages and a highly decentralized government, has been held together by a centuries-old requirement that every man serve in the army. The Swiss system not only brings men of all social classes together; it gives everybody a chance to rise to a position of leadership in both military and civilian life. Gary Hart adds that universal military training would awaken a dormant sense of patriotism in Americans, especially the young.

- **Is paying high taxes enough of a contribution to the country's defense?**

Military life is one of discipline, physical training, and education. A stint in the armed forces might steer some young Americans away from a life of crime and drugs. David

Hackworth believes that some young people need the military as much as it needs them: "Their families and schools have failed them by not instilling discipline, values, and standards. Drugs, crime, a damaged belief system, and sick entertainment industry have produced a lost generation in need of structure and salvage damn fast."[39]

- Should judges order young lawbreakers to join the military or else go to jail?

Hackworth and others see military service as a means of

What Would Happen in a Draft

According to the Selective Service System, this is the sequence of events leading up to the reinstatement of the draft:

New Selective Service Law. A crisis occurs that requires more manpower than volunteers can provide. Congress passes a resolution reinstating the draft and the president signs it.

Draft Lottery. The Selective Service System holds a lottery, based on birthdate, which determines who will be called first. The men most vulnerable to the draft are 19-year-olds. If there are not enough men of that age to fill manpower requirements, men turning 20 through 24 will be called, youngest first. Unless the nation faces a serious threat, 18-year-olds will not be drafted, nor will men 21 or older who had high lottery numbers and were not taken.

Evaluation of Draft-Age Men. Immediately after the lottery, men with low numbers will be ordered to report for a physical and mental evaluation, which will determine their fitness to serve. A man found fit will be given 10 days either to appeal his status or to ask for more time before being inducted.

Classification and Appeal. Fewer draft-age men will avoid military service than during the Vietnam-era draft. Local draft boards and appeal boards will decide requests for exemptions, deferments, and postponements.

making Americans healthier and more physically fit. During the draft era, a third of those examined were rejected because they could not meet the military's physical standards. During World War II and Vietnam, the high rejection rate was blamed on poverty. Today there is another reason: Many young people are in poor physical shape because of an unhealthy diet and lack of exercise. Supporters of universal military training point out that it would provide physical conditioning for out-of-shape recruits. Some draftees might also benefit from training they could not get as civilians. As a congressman, former United Nations (UN) Ambassador Andrew Young

Men whose appeals are denied will be ordered to report for induction. The Selective Service System intends to use the following system, which it insists will be fairer:

Class I

1-A: Available immediately for military service.

1-O: Conscientious objector opposed to all military service and available for civilian alternative service.

1-A-O: Conscientious objector available for noncombatant military service.

Class II

2-D: Deferment for ministry students.

Class III

3-A: Hardship deferment.

Class IV

4-C: Exemption of some non-U.S. citizens and holders of citizenship from both the United States and another country.

4-D: Exemption for ministers of religion.

Inductions. By law, the Selective Service must deliver the first inductees to the military within 193 days after the draft is reinstated.

Source: Selective Service System (*http://www.sss.gov*).

favored keeping the draft because the military was the only place where poor African-American men could get an education.

- **Should the military be concerned with improving soldiers' lot in life?**

Finally, the inequities of the Vietnam era do not mean that the draft should never be tried again. For most of its existence, the draft was considered fair. As Charles Moskos points out,

> We tend to forget that the more equitable draft that existed during World War II and for 20 years afterwards helped bring the country together. . . . This shared experience helped instill in those who served, as in the national culture generally, a sense of unity and moral seriousness that we would not see again—until after September 11, 2001.[40]

- **Has the national mood changed since the September 11 attacks? Has it changed for the better or for the worse?**

Our government has learned from past mistakes. It abolished the practice of commutation, placed the draft system under civilian control and created local draft boards, and switched to a system under which the youngest men were called first and selected by lottery. In a future draft, the Selective Service System intends to eliminate controversial deferments that allowed well-off men to avoid serving.

Americans Are Avoiding the Obligations of Citizenship.

Americans sometimes forget the price of freedom because, unlike the nations of continental Europe, we have never suffered an enemy occupation of our homeland. The September 11 terror attacks, however—the first enemy attack since Pearl Harbor to cause mass casualties on American soil—were a reminder of the obligation to defend our country. The Hoover Institution's Stanley Kurtz believes those attacks underscored the need for some form of a draft:

> [It] would cultivate the much-needed sense that we owe some debt of service to our country. And these cultural changes matter, for without the will to fight, our military might counts for little. For too long now, we've indulged the fantasy that we can have our way in the world without cost. Our readiness has suffered significantly as a result.[41]

- **Are Americans taking the threat of terrorism seriously?**

Conservatives and liberals alike complain that Americans pay too much attention to their rights and have forgotten that citizenship involves obligations as well. Some even question whether a person can be a good American without doing his or her civic duty—a duty that goes beyond obeying the law, voting, and occasionally serving on a jury. In the past, societies considered fighting for one's country not only a solemn duty but a high honor. It is a belief held by many Americans who served during World War II and the years that followed. To those men, "[I]t seemed both natural and worthwhile that their sons should also be drafted to defend the country; they believed that young men ought to perform military service for the country and were better off for doing so."[42]

- **What is the best way for Americans to give something back to their country?**

The duty to defend one's country is more than an ideal; it is essential to national survival. History has not been kind to societies that paid others to defend them. Many turned into dictatorships or empires. Citizens of the Roman Empire hired professional soldiers, even members of barbarian tribes, to fight for them; and many historians believe this was one reason why Rome fell. John McAuley Palmer's warning is still timely: "A people accustomed to let a special class defend them must sooner or later become unfit for liberty."[43]

Relying on the free market to provide manpower has resulted in a military that no longer represents the people it defends. With privileged young people no longer serving, the enlisted ranks are filled with the less fortunate, African Americans in particular.

FROM THE BENCH

United States v. *O'Brien*: Free Speech and Draft-Card Burning

During the Vietnam War, men not only had to register for the draft but also had to carry their certificate of registration, or "draft card," at all times. These cards came to symbolize the draft, and burning them was one way of protesting both the draft and the war. However, it was also an act of civil disobedience punishable by a prison term and a heavy fine.

In 1966, David O'Brien burned his draft card on the steps of a Boston courthouse. He was charged with willfully mutilating and destroying his draft card, in violation of the Selective Service Act (50 U.S. Code App. §462[b]). O'Brien appealed, claiming that Congress had added the ban on "mutilating and destroying" cards in 1965 as a way to punish antiwar protesters.

O'Brien's appeal went up to the Supreme Court, which, by a 7–1 vote, affirmed his conviction in *United States* v. *O'Brien*, 391 U.S. 367 (1968). Chief Justice Earl Warren's majority opinion concluded that the law prohibiting draft-card burning was constitutional. He stated that:

> A law prohibiting destruction of Selective Service certificates no more abridges free speech on its face than a motor vehicle law prohibiting the destruction of drivers' licenses, or a tax law prohibiting the destruction of books and records.

Giving a broad interpretation to Congress's military powers, Warren set out the constitutional basis for a law against mutilating or destroying draft cards:

> The constitutional power of Congress to raise and support armies and to make all laws necessary and proper to that end is broad and sweeping. . . . The power of Congress to classify and conscript manpower for military service is "beyond question". . . . Pursuant to this

In the post-draft era, the burden of defending the country is shared unequally, which is not only unfair but could have serious consequences for the nation. A draft could reunite an increasingly fragmented country and rekindle a spirit of patriotism. It also would serve as a reminder that American citizenship involves obligations as well as rights.

power, Congress may establish a system of registration for individuals liable for training and service, and may require such individuals within reason to cooperate in the registration system.... The many functions performed by Selective Service certificates establish beyond doubt that Congress has a legitimate and substantial interest in preventing their wanton and unrestrained destruction and assuring their continuing availability by punishing people who knowingly and willfully destroy or mutilate them.

The Chief Justice drew a distinction between O'Brien's opposition to the war and his act of destroying his draft card:

In conclusion, we find that because of the Government's substantial interest in assuring the continuing availability of issued Selective Service certificates ... and because the non-communicative impact of O'Brien's act of burning his registration certificate frustrated the Government's interest, a sufficient governmental interest has been shown to justify O'Brien's conviction.

Finally, Warren rejected O'Brien's contention that Congress's true motivation in adding the "mutilating and destroying" amendment was to target protesters:

Inquiries into congressional motives or purposes are a hazardous matter ... What motivates one legislator to make a speech about a statute is not necessarily what motivates scores of others to enact it, and the stakes are sufficiently high for us to eschew guesswork.

Source: *United States* v. *O'Brien*, 391 U.S. 367 (1968)

Reviving the Draft Would Do More Harm Than Good

The Defense Department has repeatedly resisted calls to bring back the draft, insisting that it neither needs nor wants draftees. That stance has not convinced everybody. Some intellectuals and lawmakers insist that the Pentagon refuses to admit that it has a manpower problem. They also believe that a draft would make the United States a more just and virtuous nation. Those who want the military to remain all volunteers disagree, however. They see the draft as a form of social engineering that would create even worse problems than those it is intended to solve. They also fear that the draft would reawaken the social turmoil of the Vietnam years.

- Can the military teach a young person values he or she never learned at home?

The Draft Is Inherently Unfair.

During the 1960s, many young Americans saw the draft as a symbol of unfairness. Criticism of the draft system led to reform and, eventually, an all-volunteer military. If there is another draft, Selective Service officials promise it will be fairer than it was during Vietnam. Any system other than universal military training, though, would lead to charges of unfairness because not all of those eligible would serve. Even during World War II, millions of draft-age men did not serve because they failed the physical exam, worked in a defense plant, or had children.

There is little chance that there will be a mobilization on the scale of World War II. If a draft does become necessary, it is likely that the number of troops needed by the military would be a small fraction of the draft-age population. A draft that takes in so few is bound to be viewed as arbitrary and is likely to produce resentment. As Professor Eliot Cohen pointed out, "Once you are no longer drafting 50 percent of the eligible population, you start to run into real equity problems. It happened here during the Vietnam War."[44]

• **Will a future draft be fairer than those of the twentieth century?**

A future draft will be based on a lottery system, which many consider a fair method of choosing who must serve. However, a lottery only decides which men are called, not who is eligible in the first place. In every previous draft, millions of men were kept out of the draft pool because of deferments. Even during World War II, special interests used their influence in Washington to get deferments for millions of men working on farms and in factories. The decision of whether to give deferments was left to draft boards, which had a considerable amount of discretion. The number-one reason for deferring men has been hardship—drafting them would cost their families their primary source of income—and the Selective Service System intended to allow hardship deferments in a future draft. The draft system's unfairness goes beyond deferments. In previous wars, better-educated men were often assigned to desk jobs in the Pentagon or in civilian organizations involved with the war effort. Human nature being what it is, the military is not immune to outside influence. During the draft era, well-connected parents got their sons into the reserves or had them assigned to less hazardous active duty.

> • **Who should be exempted from military service? Women? Fathers? Those who have lost loved ones in combat?**

The All-Volunteer Force Has Not Led to Disastrous Consequences.

An often-heard criticism of the all-volunteer military is that it

Vietnam-Era Draft Classifications

By definition, "selective service" means not all eligible men are drafted. For reasons ranging from unfitness to serve to the national interest, men are rejected or excused from the military. During the early 1960s, a growing pool of manpower meant that fewer draft-age men were actually drafted; the rest were exempted, deferred, or simply not called.

When the Vietnam War escalated, however, higher draft calls led to complaints that the classification system made minorities and the poor more likely to be drafted. Widespread criticism of the draft led to reform of the Selective Service and, finally, to the end of the draft.

During the Vietnam era, the Selective Service System used the following classification system.

Class I
1-A: Available immediately for military service.
1-A-O: Conscientious objector available for noncombatant military service.
1-C: Member of the armed forces.
1-D: Reservist or student enrolled in the Reserve Officers Training Corps (ROTC).
1-S: High school student under 20 or a college student deferred until the end of his academic year.

would become an "underclass army" dominated by those unable to find civilian jobs. However, Sue Berryman, who has studied the makeup of the military, found that enlistees "do not come from the more marginal groups on any of four dimensions: family socio-economic status, measured verbal and quantitative abilities, educational achievement, or work orientation."[45] It is even debatable whether the draft-era military was more representative than today's force. During the Vietnam War, economist Milton Friedman wrote: "A large fraction of the poor are rejected on physical and mental grounds. The relatively well-to-do are in an especially good position to take advantage of the possibilities of deferment offered by continuing their schooling. Hence the

1-W:	Conscientious objector performing civilian work.
1-Y:	Draftable only in time of war or national emergency.

Class II

II-A:	Occupational deferment.
II-C:	Agricultural deferment.
II-S:	Student deferment (which would remain in effect during satisfactory progress toward a degree).

Class III

III-A:	Extreme hardship or fatherhood deferment.

Class IV

IV-A:	Sole surviving son.
IV-B:	Public official.
IV-C:	Non-U.S. citizen not currently obligated to serve.
IV-D:	Minister of religion or divinity student.
IV-F:	Not qualified for any military service ("physically, mentally, or morally unfit").

Class V

V-A:	Too old to be drafted (generally, 26 or older or, for those given deferments, 35 or older).

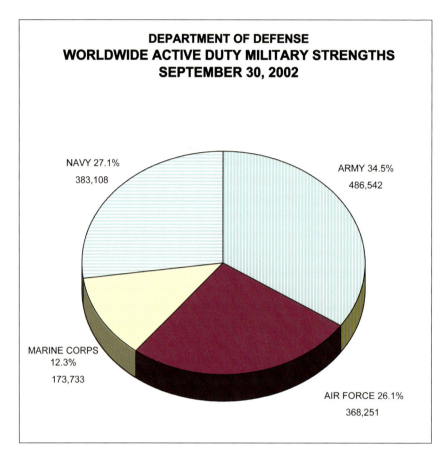

DEPARTMENT OF DEFENSE
WORLDWIDE ACTIVE DUTY MILITARY STRENGTHS
SEPTEMBER 30, 2002

NAVY 27.1%
383,108

ARMY 34.5%
486,542

MARINE CORPS
12.3%

173,733

AIR FORCE 26.1%
368,251

The different branches of the American military serve in different roles as the United States carries out its obligations at home and overseas. This pie chart prepared by the Department of Defense illustrates the overall strength of each branch of the armed forces throughout the world, as reported on September 30, 2002.

draft bears disproportionately on the upper lower classes and the lower middle class."[46]

• **Can the military ever truly be representative of the nation?**

Although there are fewer college graduates in the enlisted ranks today than during the draft era, the military as a whole—

including reservists and the officer corps—does represent the nation. The Defense Department insists that all segments of society are represented: "[I]f you look at the classes at our military academies—West Point, Annapolis, Colorado Springs—many people would argue you're looking at a future power elite there. And these are young men and young women who are quite willing to put their lives on the line, and do so."[47]

There is a high percentage of African-American enlisted personnel because African Americans reenlist at a higher rate than do whites or Hispanics. A Defense Department official explained: "There is widespread conviction that because [the military is] merit-based, African Americans, at least in terms of recent history, decide this is a good place to make a career; 'I will get a good deal out of this. I'll be judged on my abilities, not on my background.'"[48] Pentagon statistics also show that African-American soldiers are better educated—and earn more—than their civilian counterparts.

Opponents of the all-volunteer military also warned that civilian leaders would lose control of it. However, that has not happened. Civilian control of the military is a long-standing Anglo-American tradition; neither Great Britain nor the United States has ever experienced a military coup. Furthermore, there are provisions in the Constitution aimed at ensuring civilian control: The president, a civilian, is commander-in-chief of the military; and Congress has to approve the military's budget.

- **Is a military filled with "lifers" dangerous?**

A Draft Would Divide and Disrupt the Nation.

Even if a draft would save money and provide manpower, the nation would pay a high price for bringing it back. First of all, a draft would hurt the nation's economy. During the Vietnam War, young men made decisions with an eye toward reducing their chances of being called. The Gates Commission found that: "They enter college when they otherwise would not. They stay in

(Continued on page 68)

FROM THE BENCH

Clay v. *United States:* Muhammad Ali's Conscientious-Objection Fight

The most celebrated draft case in American history involved former boxing champion Muhammad Ali. Born Cassius Marcellus Clay, Ali became involved with an African-American Muslim organization, the Nation of Islam, while he was a teenager. He converted to the Muslim faith in 1964, just before winning the world heavyweight title.

At first, the military rejected Ali because of his low aptitude test score. In 1965, though, after the Pentagon lowered entry standards, his draft board reclassified him as available for immediate service. Ali then applied for conscientious-objector status based on his religious beliefs.

To qualify as a conscientious objector, Ali had to meet three tests: He had to be conscientiously opposed to war "in any form," his opposition had to be based on religious training and belief, and his opposition had to be sincere. Ali's draft board and, later, the State Appeal Board, turned him down. The Appeal Board's decision was influenced by a letter from the Justice Department concluding that Ali had not met the requirements for conscientious-objector status.

In 1967, Ali was ordered to report for induction. After he refused to take the traditional step forward, boxing commissions in New York and several other states revoked his license, and federal authorities charged him with violating the Selective Service Act. He was convicted and given the maximum sentence—five years in prison and a $10,000 fine. Some believed the harsh sentence was motivated by politics; most Americans were angered by the Nation of Islam's extreme views on race relations.

Ali appealed his conviction to a federal appeals court, which upheld it. He then asked the Supreme Court to review his case. The High Court was reluctant to take it, reportedly because of the political repercussions of such a ruling.

As his appeal made its way through the courts, Ali ran up huge legal bills. Unable to earn a living, he faced the prospect of bankruptcy. At the same time, though, public opinion began to turn against the Vietnam War, and some Americans sympathized with him. After some complicated legal maneuvering, the Supreme Court finally decided on Ali's appeal.

The Court found a face-saving way out, thanks to the Justice Department's change of position. On appeal, the government conceded that Ali's claim was based on his religious beliefs and that he was sincere. However, it continued to argue that Ali was not opposed to war in any form, but "only selectively opposed to specific wars."

On June 28, 1971, in *Clay* v. *United States*, 403 U.S. 698 (1971), the High Court unanimously reversed Ali's conviction. The justices found it unnecessary to decide whether Ali was opposed to war "in any form" because it concluded the Appeal Board had failed to spell out the reason why it denied his appeal. As a result, there was "absolutely no way of knowing upon which of the three grounds offered in the [Justice Department's] letter it relied." Since the Appeal Board's decision could have been based upon a wrong interpretation of the law, Ali's Selective Service Act conviction could not stand.

Justice William Douglas was not completely satisfied. He raised the issue of whether conscientious-objector status could be based on opposition to a specific war. Douglas observed:

> While there are some bits of evidence showing conscientious objection to the Vietnam conflict, [Ali's] basic objection was based on the teachings of his religion. The jihad is the Moslem's counterpart of the "just" war as it has been known in the West....
>
> What Clay's testimony adds up to is that he believes only in war as sanctioned by the Koran, that is to say, a religious war against nonbelievers. All other wars are unjust.

The Supreme Court never decided that issue. Some legal experts believe that a future court might find a right of "selective conscientious objection."

In 1970, Ali returned to the boxing ring. His first fight was in Georgia, a state that did not require a boxing license. Later, a court ruled that New York's boxing commission had unlawfully revoked his license because it allowed hundreds of other convicted felons—but not Ali—to fight. Several months after that court's decision, Ali met and lost to defending champion Joe Frazier. In a 1974 rematch, though, Ali beat Frazier and won the heavyweight title. After the fight, the man once denounced as a traitor was invited to visit the White House.

(Continued from page 65)

school longer than they otherwise would. They accept employment in positions they otherwise would not take. They marry and have families before they otherwise would. There is no doubt that the costs of these distorted choices are real and often cruelly high."[49]

The commission estimated that for every dollar's worth of labor the nation got from draftees, it paid $2.50 in costs, mostly because of economic distortions caused by young men's draft-conscious choices. Furthermore, the draft would be expensive to enforce. During Vietnam, an estimated half million men disobeyed the law, creating a huge workload for federal prosecutors. Some predict even greater noncompliance with a future draft because conscription has not been a part of most Americans' lives.

> • **What would you do to avoid being drafted? Marry someone you did not love? Change your career plans? Lie to the draft board?**

The draft would have a high social cost as well. It would force the nation to revisit sensitive issues such as whether to accept gays and women in the military, whether parents should be given special treatment, and what should be done with those who oppose war on religious grounds. Drafting young men for an unpopular war could divide and weaken the nation. The framers realized that sending draftees to fight far from home was unnatural and, for that reason, limited the president's power to call up the militia. Sending draftees overseas could cause social unrest; it happened in the United States during Vietnam. It also happened in France, which sent draftees to fight in Algeria in the 1960s. Some believe that reviving the draft would increase the chances of another unpopular conflict. They argue that the Vietnam War lasted so long because President Johnson relied on draftees instead of calling up the reserves. They cite another reason why a draft could lead to a war like Vietnam: It might encourage the Pentagon to waste troops on foolish missions.

As former Navy Secretary Richard Danzig observes, "When it receives people at no cost, the military, like most institutions when this happens, tends to treat them as if they were virtually of no worth."[50] Generals who thought they had an endless supply of manpower fought the bloody battles of the Civil War and the horrible war of attrition on the Western Front in World War I.

- **How much should public opinion count in making foreign policy decisions?**

The Draft Is Contrary to American Beliefs and Traditions.

Some believe that America's role as the world's policeman, which could lead to the return of the draft, is contrary to our nation's traditions. In their view, sending troops to topple the rulers of far-off countries is behavior more appropriate for an empire than a republic. They point out that the framers believed the military's proper role was to defend the homeland, not to go on overseas expeditions. For much of the nation's history, citizens and their leaders were reluctant to get involved in foreign wars—a major reason why there has been a draft for only 35 of the 200-plus years since independence. If the military is overworked, which has been another argument for reinstating the draft, critics blame wasteful overseas commitments such as peacekeeping missions in Bosnia and Kosovo. Some people even argue that America's overseas presence encourages terrorism. The Hoover Institution's Thomas Gale Moore points out: "Wherever we have bases, the local population resents those troops. . . . American troops abroad furnish both a motivation for terrorism and a target."[51]

- **Should the military be doing work that might be better left to police agencies?**

Although the framers believed every man had a duty to defend his country, they viewed military service as a necessary evil. During the last few decades, some Americans have started to question whether the draft is even justifiable. Defying centuries-old beliefs, Milton Friedman examined the economic consequences of the draft and concluded that it was an ineffi- cient and unjust tax. At the same time, thinkers on both ends of the political spectrum started asking whether it was even moral for the state to command people to serve it. One such thinker, Doug Bandow, believes that "Conscription would undermine the very individual liberty that makes our nation worth defending."[52] Former President Reagan was even more outspoken:

> [The draft] rests on the assumption that your kids belong to the state. If we buy that assumption then it is for the state—not for parents, the community, the religious insti- tutions, or teachers—to decide who shall have what values and who shall do what work, when, where, and how in our society. That assumption isn't a new one. The Nazis thought it was a great idea.[53]

• **Does the government have any business telling citizens what to do for a living?**

Over the years, the draft has been associated with tyrants. The worst regimes of the last century, from Adolf Hitler's Germany to Saddam Hussein's Iraq, relied on the draft to raise large armies. Dictators are fond of conscription because it gives them control over the nation's young men. As the Discovery Institute's Bruce Chapman observes, "Outside of mass mobiliza- tion for war—or in the special case of Israel, a small nation effectively on constant alert—the only modern nations that have conscripted labor to meet assorted, centrally decreed social purposes have been totalitarian regimes."[54]

Although the United States is far from a dictatorship, some analysts, such as Robert Higgs of the Independent Institute, believe it hardly resembles the republic the founders had in mind. In Higgs's view, the draft deserves much of the blame for the growth of government power: "If the draft is acceptable, then X is acceptable, X being any form of government coercion whatsoever. . . . Even the Supreme Court adopted the argument, as Justice Hugo Black evinced in a 1942 decision: 'Congress can draft men for battle service. Its power to draft business organizations to support the fighting men who risk their lives can be no less.'"[55]

Finally, the American people are on the whole against bringing back the draft. In January 2003, as the nation prepared for war with Iraq, a CNN/*USA Today*/Gallup poll found only 27 percent of Americans in favor of a draft, compared to 69 percent against.

- **Has the government become too powerful? Does it tax and spend too much?**

Whatever benefits the nation would realize from a draft would be more than outweighed by the resulting costs to society. No draft system is completely fair, and rich or powerful Americans would find a way to avoid being called. Furthermore, the dire consequences of an all-volunteer military, including an "underclass army" and military commanders who defy civilian control, have not happened. Reviving the draft could divide Americans by forcing them to debate emotional issues, such as whether women and gays should serve. It also could make it easier for a future president to start an unpopular war like Vietnam. Finally, the draft violates many Americans' belief in limited government.

Even Without a Draft, a National Service Require-ment Would Benefit Society

O ne alternative to a draft is a requirement that young Americans perform nonmilitary service to their country. Though there never has been such a requirement in the United States, it has been under serious discussion since William James's essay "The Moral Equivalent of War" first appeared in 1906. James, a pacifist, proposed "drafting" men to do hard work that would channel their warlike instincts into projects that benefited others. During the Vietnam War, some lawmakers proposed national service as a way of making the draft less unfair. More recently, scholars and political leaders have revived the idea. Some of its strongest advocates belong to the Democratic Leadership Council, a group whose best-known member is former President Clinton. Backers can be found in both political parties, however. Supporters of national service see it as a way for young people to "pay their dues" to society.

Unlike James's original idea, many current proposals would apply to women as well as men and would allow participants to serve in either a civilian or a military capacity.

- **What can be done to redirect humans' warlike urges into something more constructive?**

Society Has Serious Unmet Needs.

As prosperous as the United States is, millions of citizens need help and cannot get it. These people have "fallen through the cracks" because, as the Democratic Leadership Council explains, "Neither the public nor private sector has the means or will to undertake innumerable tasks that have low profit but high civic value." [56] Many of these tasks are labor-intensive, require few specialized skills, and would be prohibitively expensive if workers were paid the going rate. National service advocates consider such work well suited for young people, who are capable of doing physical tasks and have fewer family obligations.

- **Is it fair to expect young people to serve their country when most of their parents never did?**

A number of unmet needs have been identified. One is providing health care and other services for the elderly, the nation's fastest-growing population group. Another is caring for the children of the millions of women, many of them single mothers, who must work to support their families. Yet another is supporting the schools, which could use thousands of tutors, mentors, and teacher's aides. Other projects for national service participants include maintaining parks and recreation areas, staffing libraries and museums, and building housing.

- **Which do a better job of helping the poor: government agencies or private charities?**

Supporters concede that a national service program would not be cheap. However, they see it as an investment similar to the GI Bill. They also believe that its benefits would more than offset its costs. Robert Litan cites a 1995 General Accounting Office study concluding that every dollar invested in the national service program AmeriCorps yielded between $1.68 and $2.58 in benefits to society. Litan goes on to say: "These estimates did not count the nonquantifiable, but very real, benefits of strengthening local communities and fostering civic responsibility. Nor did

"The Moral Equivalent of War" by William James

Philosopher William James was one of the first American thinkers to promote the idea of national service. Although he was a pacifist, James realized that war sometimes brought out the best in men. His essay, "The Moral Equivalent of War," was an attempt to promote the military virtues of courage, self-sacrifice, and teamwork without going to war.

James conceded that war has been, and is, part of human nature:

> We inherit the warlike type; and for most of the capacities of heroism that the human race is full of we have to thank this cruel history.... Our ancestors have bred pugnacity into our bone and marrow, and thousands of years of peace won't breed it out of us....
>
> Militarism is the great preserver of our ideals of hardihood, and human life with no use for hardihood would be contemptible. Without risks or prizes for the darer, history would be insipid indeed; and there is a type of military character which every one feels that the race should never cease to breed, for everyone is sensitive to its superiority.

He criticized his fellow pacifists for failing to come up with some way to redirect humans' warlike impulses:

> So long as antimilitarists propose no substitute for war's disciplinary function, no *moral equivalent* of war, analogous, as one might say, to the mechanical equivalent of heat, so long they fail to realize the full inwardness of the situation. And as a rule they do fail. The duties,

they include the broader benefits of added social cohesion that a universal program would entail."[57]

National Service Would Strengthen the Country.

Supporters believe that national service is a way to bring Americans back together without the social disruption that a war, or even a peacetime draft, would bring about. In Robert

penalties, and sanctions pictured in the utopias they paint are all too weak and tame to touch the military-minded.

James believed that even if war could be eliminated, nations would still have to function with much of the physical discipline associated with the military:

We must make new energies and hardihoods continue the manliness to which the military mind so faithfully clings. Martial virtues must be the enduring cement; intrepidity, contempt of softness, surrender of private interest, obedience to command, must still remain the rock upon which states are built.

Turning to specifics, James proposed drafting young men to perform hard and dangerous — but rewarding — work on behalf of others:

If now — and this is my idea — there were, instead of military conscription, a conscription of the whole youthful population to form for a certain number of years a part of the army enlisted against *Nature*, the injustice would tend to be evened out. . . .

Such a conscription . . . would preserve in the midst of a pacific civilization the manly virtues which the military party is so afraid of seeing disappear in peace. We should get toughness without callousness, authority with as little criminal cruelty as possible, and painful work done cheerily because the duty is temporary.

Source: *http://www.emory.edu/EDUCATION/mfp/moral.html*

Litan's opinion, national service would provide "social glue" for a nation "that is growing increasingly diverse—by race, national origin, and religious preference—and where many young Americans from well-to-do families grow up and go to school in hermetically sealed environments."[58] Litan adds, "For many people, their year in compulsory service may be the only time in their lives where they mix for an extended period of time and on an equal footing with others from very different backgrounds."[59]

> • **How important is it for people to live and work with those who are different from themselves?**

What distinguishes national service from most jobs is its "civic value"—that is, the server is rewarded by doing work that is important to the rest of society. During the Great Depression, the federal government created the Civilian Conservation Corp (CCC), which employed young men from poor families. Two million CCC men worked together on projects such as planting trees, building roads, and fighting soil erosion. They not only had paying jobs that helped support their families, but they also took pride in knowing they had done something worthwhile for their fellow Americans.

> • **Do today's young people have it too easy? Or must they deal with problems their parents never had to face?**

Advocates of national service also believe it could strengthen "civic society," the network of church-based and non-profit organizations that help the less fortunate. Many of those institutions are struggling because people, for reasons ranging from busy work schedules to in-home entertainment, have become less involved in civic and charitable work. Supporters believe that national service could help reconnect young people with their communities. Some even see it becoming a "contract among the generations," much like Social Security. Young people would serve with the expectation of being helped later in life by future generations.

During the Great Depression, Franklin Roosevelt's administration implemented programs such as the Civilian Conservation Corp (CCC) to give young people an opportunity to find jobs as well as to help the country by working on public service projects. This poster encourages young men to join the CCC, highlighting the many benefits participation in the CCC provides.

Those who favor a national service requirement also contend it would improve the character of those who serve. William James believed that by taking time off from college and doing hard work, well-to-do young men would "get the childishness knocked out of them, and come back into society with healthier sympathies and soberer ideas."[60] Although his notions of manliness might be outdated, James makes a good point: A year or two spent helping others would leave participants with better work habits and greater self-discipline. National service might even prevent young people from destroying their lives. According to Phil Keisling, Oregon's former secretary of state: "Many of our young people succumb to too-early parenthood, to drug and alcohol abuse, to gangs and violence. National service obviously won't be a panacea. But it can communicate a powerful message that often isn't received by our younger citizens—that you can make a difference. Society values your contribution."[61]

- **What would you do to make Americans healthier? Is universal military training part of your solution?**

It also has been argued that national service would enrich young people's education. Both the school day and school year have become longer, and a growing percentage of Americans go on to college and graduate school. While they spend more time in class, though, they are getting less exposure to the "real world" of work and community life. Experts are concerned that today's schools pay too much attention to grades and test scores and not enough to one's ability to function as a citizen. As Professor Morris Janowitz explains,

[T]he recent increased academic effectiveness of the American educational system, especially at the high school level, has been purchased at the price of complicating the process of personal development. In a democratic society it is particularly dangerous to make school and academic performance the exclusive route to mobility into adult society.[62]

Service to others is one way to keep students from developing an "ivory tower" mentality. That is why the Carnegie Foundation recommends making community service a condition of graduating both high school and college. A growing number of schools, especially at the high school level, have imposed such a requirement. Supporters also believe national service would turn participants into better-functioning students, much like the veterans who studied on the GI Bill. The time spent away from the classroom also would allow them to take a fresh look at their future and learn about career possibilities they had not considered before.

- **Has school prepared you to become an active member of your community?**

National service would help make society more equitable. Because it would be universal, society's most talented members would have to contribute—something that is not happening in the post-draft era. At the same time, it would benefit those who are not planning on college, a segment of the population that the government often neglects. The Democratic Leadership Council proposes giving participants money for job training or a down payment on a home as an alternative to college tuition. National service also would give the poor and those educated in inadequate school systems an opportunity to gain skills and start on a career path. It would also give "late bloomers" who performed poorly in school a second chance to succeed.

National Service Would Reemphasize Obligations to Society.

Many people who fought in World War II, including Presidents Dwight Eisenhower, John F. Kennedy, and George H.W. Bush, believed that a service program involving millions of young Americans would bring the nation together in much the same way that the war effort did. Members of the "Greatest Generation" considered serving their country a virtue as well as a duty. That patriotic spirit suffered during the Vietnam War, however, when many young people associated military service with an unfair and unpopular draft.

The idea that service is part of being a citizen is as old as the United States itself. In calling for universal military training, President George Washington said, "A period of civic sacrifice heightened individual disposition to loyalty, to involvement in civic affairs, and to the identification of one's own interests with those of the community."[63] National service supporters hope it can reestablish the connection between individual rights and duties owed to others. Since the Vietnam War, that connection has been broken. For example, the GI Bill offered World War II veterans a free college education. After Vietnam, student-aid programs expanded to the point that the federal government now awards $40 billion a year in grants and loans, most of it to students who never served their country and probably never will. There is still public support for the idea that the benefits of citizenship should be earned. A recent poll found a majority in favor of requiring young people to perform a year of national service. Some even believe that privileged Americans have a stronger obligation to serve. This approach is followed in some other countries: Costa Rica and Mexico, for example, require medical students to complete a year of service in impoverished areas.

- **Should veterans get preferences for government jobs and benefits?**

The end of the draft is not the only reason why fewer young people now serve their country. Senator John McCain finds opportunities for service disappearing, even for the willing: "The high cost of campaigning keeps many idealistic people from running for public office. Teacher-certification requirements keep talented people out of the classroom. The all-volunteer military is looking for lifers, not those who might want to serve for shorter tours of duty."[64]

Another argument in favor of national service is that it would help reverse a national trend toward selfishness. Supporters believe that those who begin serving at an early age develop a lifelong habit of helping others, just as military veterans often got involved in their communities after they came home. In the words of political commentator William F. Buckley, "At age 21 the [national service] veteran, his certificate in his pocket, is not likely to forget that there are old, lonely people out there, families who need day care, illiterates who need coaching, streets that need cleaning, forest fires that need fighting."[65]

• **Most consider the GI Bill a successful government program. Can you think of other successes?**

National Service Is Fairer Than the Draft.

Even if the draft is reinstated, chances are that only a fraction of military-age men would be called—a situation that would once again raise questions of fairness. A national service requirement, on the other hand, would be more inclusive and therefore more equitable. If everybody had to take part, the program would not suffer from the arbitrariness of a lottery or biased decisions on the part of draft boards.

• **Is a universal military training requirement fairer than a draft lottery?**

There is a good chance that a national service requirement would apply to both sexes. There would be less opposition to including women because they would not be sent into combat. Fewer people would be rejected because the physical and mental standards for national service would be less demanding than those of the military. Even men and women with physical disabilities or below-average intelligence could be given some kind of assignment. One expert foresees a rejection rate of 10 percent, compared to one-third during the draft era. There also would be fewer people excused from serving: Student and occupational deferments would not exist; and, because a national service assignment would be shorter, fewer people would be exempted on account of hardship.

- **Does the military's high rejection rate indicate that Americans are too "soft"?**

A national service requirement could benefit the military as well. The Democratic Leadership Council believes it would encourage civic-mindedness, which, in turn, would spur recruitment and strengthen the citizen-soldier tradition. Faced with the obligation to serve for a year or more, young people—including the college-bound—would be more likely to consider a military option, especially if short tours of duty were offered and veterans could earn GI Bill benefits. Requiring everyone to serve in some capacity also would eliminate one current obstacle to recruiting: Those who volunteer suffer a disadvantage because they delay their education or career by several years. National service would also make the military more efficient by providing a corps of trained civilians who could respond to terror attacks and natural disasters. If national service participants are assigned to homeland-security duties, such as border and airport security, regular soldiers would be available for more critical missions.

As prosperous as this country is, millions of needy Americans are not being helped by government programs or private charities. A national service program for young people would address these unmet needs. It also would give Americans the opportunity to fulfill their duties of citizenship. At the same time, it would unite the country by bringing together people from different backgrounds. Since national service would be universal, it would suffer few of the problems that made the Vietnam-era draft unpopular. Under models of mandatory service that would include program options like AmeriCorps and jobs dealing with homeland security, national service would give participants real-world skills to round out their classroom learning, and it would leave them better prepared for college and work.

A National Service Requirement Is Unnecessary and Unfair

S upporters of national service believe it would revive the notion that citizens owe a duty to their country and that it would benefit participants as well as society. Opponents counter that national service is an expensive social experiment that could lead to unexpected results. Americans have a long tradition of donating time and money to worthy causes; over the years, they have created thousands of nonprofit and religious organizations that help those in need. National service would duplicate the work of existing charities, and it might even replace them with a less-efficient government bureaucracy. Even worse, national service would expand the government's power by requiring citizens to render service even when national survival was not threatened.

National Service Would Be Expensive and Hard to Administer.

Universal national service never has been tried in this country. There are good reasons why. To begin with, it would be an enormous undertaking. It would require creating a huge government agency to oversee the program and hiring thousands of employees to train and keep track of participants. Those participants would number in the millions. Each year, about 4 million Americans turn 18. Assuming that all of them must serve for a year, there would be more people in the national service program than in the active duty military and the reserves combined. A program of that size would be, of course, costly. According to the Discovery Institute's Bruce Chapman,

> [T]he direct costs of a national-service program would include those for assembling, sorting (and sorting out), allocating, and training several million youth in an unending manpower convoy. Indirect costs include clothing and providing initial medical attention, insurance, the law enforcement associated with such large numbers (no small expense in the army, even with presumably higher discipline), housing, and the periodic "leave" arrangements.[66]

- **The all-volunteer military was an experiment that worked. Why not experiment with national service?**

Estimates run as high as $120 billion a year, an investment many consider questionable at best. Chapman estimates that national service would cost $30,000 a year per participant—an amount higher than entry-level pay in many fields.

Turnover would be a major problem in a national service program. Most proposals call for a year or 18 months of service, an even shorter assignment than a military draftee's two-year tour of duty. Participants would have relatively little time to learn and get used to their jobs before their obligation would

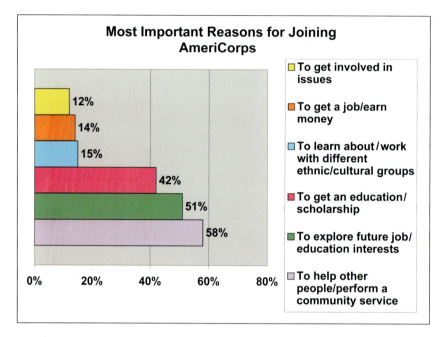

Most Important Reasons for Joining AmeriCorps

- ☐ To get involved in issues
- ☐ To get a job/earn money
- ☐ To learn about/work with different ethnic/cultural groups
- ☐ To get an education/ scholarship
- ☐ To explore future job/ education interests
- ☐ To help other people/perform a community service

12%
14%
15%
42%
51%
58%

0%   20%   40%   60%   80%

Advocates of mandatory national service programs cite a sense of self-esteem and patriotism as a benefit of participation. This graph, which uses data provided by AmeriCorps, one of the nation's most popular service programs, shows volunteers' responses to questions about the value of service experience.

come to an end. Another problem would be unqualified workers. National service assignments would run the gamut from tutoring third-graders to providing in-home care for Alzheimer's patients. Many would involve direct contact with people in need. Giving a person an assignment for which he or she was unsuited, such as caring for children, could do more harm than good. The same could be even truer of those with homeland-security assignments. The Cato Institute's Doug Bandow warns: "Conscripting 18-year-olds would do nothing to protect America from terrorism; a few skilled personnel can do far more to make us safe than masses of untrained young people."[67] Finally, there is the problem of motivation: The national service program, like the draft-era military, would have unwilling participants who would perform accordingly.

- **Is it more difficult to train people to serve others than to teach them to fight?**

A national service program could damage other institutions in society. Charitable organizations are especially vulnerable. They might be pressured to accept national service workers whose services they do not need. In the long run, government-sponsored programs might compete with charities and eventually displace them, leaving those in need even worse off than before. National service even might tempt political leaders to scale back government antipoverty programs that have existed for years. As E.J. Dionne and Kayla Meltzer Drogosz observe, "Citizenship cannot be reduced to service. And service—good works whether of faith communities, the private sector, or 'communities of character'—cannot replace the responsibilities of government." [68]

- **Do private nonprofit organizations understand people's needs better than government agencies do?**

Higher education, too, would suffer. Colleges would have to keep places open for students performing national service. Some students might have problems adjusting to academic life after a year or more of service. A national service obligation would also prevent men and women from poor families from taking a paying job to earn tuition money. There are concerns, too, that national service could hurt military recruiting, especially if civilian veterans were given generous benefits; the result might be even fewer talented people in the armed forces. National service might also set back efforts to reform the nation's education and health-care systems. If school and hospital administrators were given a steady stream of low-paid workers, they would have no incentive to become more efficient, just as the draft-era military resisted efforts to change its outdated ways.

A National Service Program Would Lead to Waste and Abuse.

A national service program would likely pay participants below-market wages, perhaps even less than the minimum wage. Some believe that the combination of underpaid labor and government bureaucracy would make waste and abuse inevitable. According to Doug Bandow:

> Turning over to Washington the lives of the 4 million men and women who turn 18 every year would guarantee the grossest misuse of enormous human potential. If opportunity cost is not considered, perceived "needs" will be infinite. Control by a federal government engaged in the usual pursuit of political pork would guarantee that national service would become a monumental boondoggle.[69]

- **Is it justifiable to pay any worker, civilian or military, less than the minimum wage?**

Becasue cheap labor would eliminate the necessity to make trade-offs among projects, the result would be a long list of unmet needs requiring national service workers. Even before the September 11 attacks, national service supporters had identified tasks that would require millions of participants.

Critics point to AmeriCorps as an example of how inefficient "federalized volunteerism" can be. Despite having a small number of participants, it has grown into a $1 billion a year program. AmeriCorps also illustrates how federal programs can be politicized. During the 1990s, conservatives accused AmeriCorps participants of organizing in support of causes such as gun control and gay rights. Liberals, too, are concerned that national service could be misused for political purposes. They worry that it could provide an excuse to cut back government services or weaken the power of labor unions. Some even

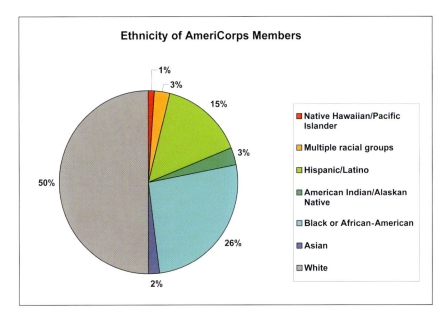

Ethnicity of AmeriCorps Members

- 1%
- 3%
- 15%
- 3%
- 50%
- 26%
- 2%

Legend:
- Native Hawaiian/Pacific Islander
- Multiple racial groups
- Hispanic/Latino
- American Indian/Alaskan Native
- Black or African-American
- Asian
- White

Although traditional mandatory service programs, such as the draft, have tended to recruit a disproportionate number of minorities, service programs that are currently voluntary, such as AmeriCorps, seem to have more diversity. This pie chart maps the ethnicity of AmeriCorps members. At 50 percent, whites are by far the largest participating group.

fear that national service would benefit the rich at the expense of those less fortunate. As Douglas Hicks warns, "We have reason to be suspicious of politicians' motives when they tout the benefits of service even as they dismantle the government-sponsored safety net."[70]

- **Should tax money ever be used to fund political activism? Even for causes such as safer highways or cleaner air?**

Opponents insist that a government-run national service program could never be as efficient as traditional charities. That is especially true because many participants would be there against their will. Requiring people to serve might have long-term negative effects as well. Some critics warn that unwilling participants could develop a distaste for service rather than a lifelong habit of helping others. As the Discovery Institute's Bruce Chapman argues,

> Does a student who learns that almost everything counts toward the service requirement—so long as he doesn't get paid—develop a keen sense of civil calling? Or does he hone his skill at gaming the system? And why, if we have this service requirement in high school—and some colleges—do we need yet another one for the year after high school?[71]

• **Can a habit of serving others be taught, or must it come from one's heart?**

Given the problems associated with mandatory national service, some believe incentives to serve would be a wiser alternative. They favor giving people information about service opportunities in their community, as well as creating and funding programs aimed at problems not addressed by existing charities. They also urge Americans to honor those who do serve, much as we honor military veterans, in the hope that service to others could one day become a "cultural rite of passage" that young people would want to be part of.

National Service Leads to the Same Objections as the Draft.

Even though most national service supporters envision a universal program, not everybody actually would participate. Though standards would be lower than those of the military, some people would be unfit or unable to serve, including those with severe physical or mental disabilities, criminal records, or serious behavioral or substance abuse problems, as well as those whose families would suffer hardship if they served. Someone would have to decide who should be excused, and those decisions could lead to charges of unfairness.

Given the sheer size of a universal program, even its supporters propose phasing it in over a period of years. During that time,
national service would be selective, raising many of the same
issues as the Vietnam-era draft. If certain categories of young
people were exempted, it would be necessary to create a bureaucracy to handle classification cases. If participants were selected by
lottery, the burden of service would fall on an unlucky few. Either
approach would cause resentment.

> • **What makes more sense: phasing in mandatory national service**
> **over five years or making it voluntary for the first five years?**

Because a universal national service program would have
many unwilling participants, it is likely it would suffer from
discipline problems. Administrators would have to decide how
to handle participants who disobey rules, fail to show up, or
turn out to be poor workers. Discharging them might provide
others with an incentive to break the rules as well, but keeping
them in the program could disrupt coworkers. There is also
the related problem of what should be done to those who
are "dishonorably discharged" from national service or
who evade their obligation in the first place. If the extent of
"draft-dodging" during the Vietnam War is any indication,
there could be widespread defiance of a national service
requirement, especially in peacetime. Some favor denying
federal benefits to those who refuse to serve. Others argue that
such a penalty might be too harsh, and add that cutting off aid
would hurt the poor more than those who are well-off.

> • **What would be an appropriate punishment for refusing to**
> **perform national service?**

National Service Is Contrary to American
Ideas of Liberty.

Requiring young people, or anyone else, to perform volunteer
work is a contradiction in terms. *Volunteer* comes from a Latin

word meaning "of one's own free will." Many Americans believe that charity, like religion, comes from the heart and cannot be imposed by the state. They also insist that mandatory civilian service is not necessary in a country with a long tradition of volunteering. As the Hoover Institution's Tod Lindbergh explains: "Americans volunteer in large numbers and give substantial sums to charitable causes—have always done so. Not because their tax returns will be scrutinized to make sure their contributions measure up, but because they want to."[72]

Is the Draft a Tax? Milton Friedman's Free-Market Argument

When the all-volunteer military was first proposed, even supporters admitted that it was a risky experiment. It was based on the radical idea that military service was not a duty or a privilege, but rather, a tax—and an unfair one at that.

The most outspoken believer that the draft was a tax was Nobel Prize–winning economist Milton Friedman. In the 1960s, his thinking influenced Richard Nixon who, as a presidential candidate, called for an end to the draft. Friedman was also an influential member of the Gates Commission, which President Nixon created to develop a plan for changing to an all-volunteer force.

In 1966, Friedman submitted a paper to a University of Chicago conference studying the future of the draft. He called the draft system "inequitable, wasteful, and inconsistent with a free society." Friedman blamed the draft's existence on bureaucrats' natural resistance to change, charging that even though manpower needs were no longer the same, the military found it easier to continue following World War II–era policies. One such policy was to underpay soldiers because they had no choice but to serve.

Friedman believed the draft existed for another reason: Military and political leaders underestimated its true cost. They failed to take into account the difference between what the military paid a draftee and the amount for which he would have served willingly. Friedman labeled that difference a tax—one that came out of the draftee's pocket. If the "draft tax" were added to the other costs

Because the primary objective of national service would be helping the needy, not defending the country, the case for making it mandatory is considered even weaker than that for a draft. According to Bruce Chapman, "The Founders had a keen awareness of the ways that the state could tyrannize the people, and taking the people's liberty away to serve some specious government purpose unattached to national survival is a project that would horrify them."[73]

Critics also believe that national service is a dishonest

of the military, he argued, an all-volunteer force would actually be cheaper, especially if higher pay forced the services to use personnel more efficiently. Friedman took particular exception to the draft because it was a "tax in kind"— one paid in the form of labor rather than money. He argued: "How can we justify . . . involuntary servitude except in times of the greatest national emergency? One of the great gains in the progress of civilization was the elimination of the power of the nobleman or the sovereign to exact compulsory servitude." Friedman also considered military recruiting a "referendum" on American foreign policy: "The popularity or unpopularity of the activities for which the Armed Forces are used will clearly affect the ease of recruiting men."

To end the draft, Friedman called on the military to improve pay and living conditions for enlisted personnel. He argued that paying soldiers less than the going rate was no different from making them pay an extra tax on their income. Friedman also believed it was essential to set a definite date for the transition to an all-volunteer force; otherwise, military commanders would continue to rely on the draft, rather than better recruiting and personnel policies, to fill their manpower needs.

Source: Milton Friedman, "Why Not a Voluntary Army?" in Sol Tax, ed., *The Draft: A Handbook of Facts and Alternatives.* Chicago: University of Chicago, 1967.

way of supporting social programs. As the Gates Commission remarked, "If the service that youth would render is important and valuable enough to merit public support, it can and should be financed through general taxation like other government programs."[74] If the draft is a tax, the same reasoning also would apply to a mandatory national service program that pays its participants below-market wages. Some might argue that the "national service tax" is less arbitrary than the draft because a higher percentage of young people would serve. On the other hand, the overall tax would be more unfair because the total amount "collected" would be greater.

> • **What is fairer: requiring young people to serve for a year or raising taxes on incomes above the national average?**

Many Americans reject the idea, advanced by national service supporters, that serving one's country should be a condition of enjoying the benefits of citizenship. Some even question whether a citizen "owes" something to a country that was founded to preserve individual liberty, personal as well as economic. There is also the question of whether the state has any business telling young people what to do with their lives. Even William F. Buckley, a supporter of national service, cautions: "[I]t used to be routine, in such societies as Stalin's, Hitler's, and Mao Tse-tung's, to tell 18-year-olds what to proceed to do: to continue with their schooling, to report for duty at a state farm, to join the army or the secret police; whatever."[75]

Finally, legal experts question whether a national service obligation would even be constitutional—at least in the absence of a draft that offered civilian service as an alternative to a tour of duty in the military. In fact, some national service proposals are coupled with some form of a draft.

• **Is national service a form of involuntary servitude? Can the same be said of mandatory community service in schools?**

Mandatory national service, which has never been tried in this country, raises a number of serious concerns. A universal program would be enormously expensive, and it likely would be plagued by waste and abuse. A short period of service would mean constant turnover and the costs that accompany it. National service probably would be less efficient than existing charities; and, being a huge government program, it could end up competing with and weakening those charities. Finally, national service is prone to the same objections as the Vietnam-era draft: It has the potential to be unfairly administered, and it offends many Americans' notions of individual liberty.

The Future of Mandatory Service

S ince 1973, Americans have not been required to serve their country. Whether that continues depends on two factors: the international situation and Americans' attitudes toward service. It is, of course, impossible to predict the future. In August 2001, few imagined that an enemy would—or even could—commit an act of war that would kill thousands of American civilians. However, it is possible to speculate about events that could lead to the revival of the draft or to the creation of a mandatory national service program.

• **Is the nation prepared to stop another terror attack?**

Looking Forward: What Could Bring Back the Draft?

The Defense Department insists that the military has enough manpower to defend the nation. Many supporters of the draft disagree. They maintain that after the Soviet Union collapsed, the United States repeated a mistake it has made after every major war: cutting the military to the point that the nation was left unprepared for the next major conflict. They also point out that the armed forces were downsized even further after the Cold War ended. Today's active duty military is one-third smaller than it was in 1989. Some see a parallel between our military and that of nineteenth-century Great Britain. The British Army was an overextended volunteer force capable of fighting brushfire wars on the fringes of the empire, but was ill prepared for the all-out fighting of World War I.

Even if the United States is not involved in a major war, observers suggest a number of situations that could force it to bring back the draft. One is a conflict with two or more countries at the same time, which would stretch the military to the limit. Even with Saddam Hussein out of power in Iraq, a number of other countries are considered threats. Another situation might be a drawn-out war in a country such as Colombia, where fighting has been going on for years, or the Congo, where the bloodiest war since World War II is taking place. Wars mean peacekeeping and nation building responsibilities afterward. American troops are still serving in Bosnia and Kosovo years after the fighting ended there, and they may be in Iraq for a long time to come. War or no war, America's military commitments may result in manpower requirements that cannot be filled by volunteers alone. This is especially true after the September 11 attacks. The military, especially National Guard troops, have been assigned to homeland-security duty, such as patrolling the skies over major cities and providing security at border crossings. The Guard, however, along with the reserves, would be called up in wartime, leaving states and cities with not enough personnel to respond to terror attacks or natural disasters.

- **Does the United States meddle too much in the affairs of foreign countries? Or have modern weapons made the whole world a concern of ours?**

Political as well as military developments could lead to the return of the draft. Some present-day Americans, like the framers of the Constitution, believe a professional army is dangerous. Former Senator Gary Hart warns: "Too few know that almost three thousand years of republican history warn against such an institution, that permanent armies have consistently been seen as antithetical to democracy."[76] Hart, along with other believers in the citizen-soldier tradition, favors universal military training to avoid the rise of a military class and to defend the homeland.

The public's current antidraft stance also could change. History shows that Americans' attitude toward service runs in cycles. Since independence from Great Britain, two competing philosophies have battled for political dominance: "The liberals viewed personal freedom as the heart of the American experiment. The civic republicans valued freedom, too, but stressed that self-rule demanded a great deal from citizens. The liberals stressed rights. The civic republicans stressed obligations to a common good."[77]

- **Do Americans pay too much attention to individual rights and not enough to the common good?**

Today, the liberal tradition is carried on by libertarians such as Milton Friedman, and the civic republican tradition is carried on by Charles Moskos and other communitarians. In recent years, political leaders have been influenced by libertarian ideas, especially a free-market approach to military service. This has not always been the case. During and after World War II, Americans held the military in high regard; men were expected to serve, and army life was part of the coming-of-age process. If the pendulum swings back in that direction, the chances of mandatory service would increase.

Questions Surrounding a Future Draft

Supporters insist that the next draft will be fairer than that of the Vietnam era. However, reinstating it would raise a number of issues that might divide the nation. The most emotional issue

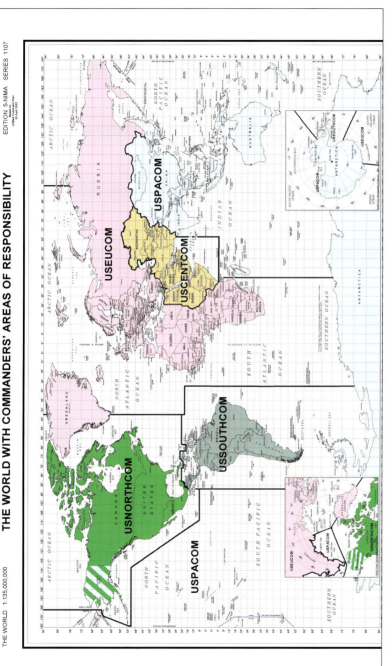

THE WORLD WITH COMMANDERS' AREAS OF RESPONSIBILITY

The United States, as the world's only superpower, has made military commitments all over the world. This map, produced by the Department of Defense, shows the areas of responsibility for different military commands. USNORTHCOM refers to the U.S. Northern Command; USPACOM stands for U.S. Pacific Command; USSOUTHCOM is U.S. Southern Command; USEUCOM refers to the U.S. European Command; and USCENTCOM refers to U.S. Central Command.

would be whether to draft women. In 1980, Congress rejected President Carter's recommendation that both sexes be required to register for the draft. There are no signs that that policy will soon change, even though women now make up 15 percent of the military, and stereotypes about women and work have been proven untrue. Both civilian and military leaders remain opposed to drafting women. In 1992, a presidential commission recommended against requiring women to register. Two years later, the Defense Department came to a similar conclusion. Nevertheless, supporters of women's rights argue that the Supreme Court's decision in *Rostker* v. *Goldberg*, 453 U.S. 57

The Draft In Other Countries

Canada. Like the United States, Canada has a strong militia tradition and a long-standing dislike of the draft. There was a draft toward the end of World War I. There was also one during World War II, but, for most of that war, draftees were assigned to homeland-defense duty in order to allow volunteers to serve overseas.

China (People's Republic). The Chinese Constitution obligates all citizens to defend their country. Under Chinese law, men are obligated to serve in the military for two years, beginning at age 18; women, too, may be drafted if necessary. Beginning in the late 1970s, China's rulers downsized the People's Liberation Army to fight modern-day wars and to shift funds from the military to the civilian economy.

France. The government of France pioneered the modern military draft after the French Revolution. The English word *conscription* comes from the name of the French system under which men were classified for service and selected by lottery—a system copied by other Western countries. After drafting men for more than two centuries, France, like Italy and Spain, has now shifted to an all-volunteer military.

Germany. Prussia, an ancestor of modern-day Germany, instituted a draft in the early nineteenth century. After World War II, the West German government brought back the draft to avoid the civilian-military divide that plagued the country before

(1981), which found male-only registration constitutional, should be overturned. Columnist Ellen Goodman argues: "[*Rostker*] was 22 years ago, before women were on the Court, before most of the restrictions were lifted, before there were 33 female generals and 212,000 female soldiers doing nearly every job in the military short of ground combat."[78]

- **Should women register for the draft? Should female draftees be sent into combat?**

A debate over the draft would force Congress and the courts to tackle the broader, and still unresolved, question of whether

(Continued on page 104)

and during Hitler's Third Reich. The German Constitutional Court recently upheld the draft, which permits young men to choose alternative civilian service.

Israel. Virtually from its founding in 1948, Israel has had a system of universal military training for men and for most women, beginning at age 18. Israeli men must serve on active duty for three years, and women for 21 months. The Israeli Defense Force, like the American military, has gradually broadened opportunities for women to serve.

Russia. Young men were subject to the draft both under the tsars and during the Soviet era. The former Soviet Union required men to serve for three years, beginning at age 18; the active duty period was also used for political indoctrination. Men in post-Soviet Russia must serve for two years. The Russian Constitution guarantees the right of conscientious objection, but Parliament has so far resisted the idea.

United Kingdom. Unlike Continental European countries, the United Kingdom has relied largely on volunteers for military manpower. It resorted to a draft in 1916 to fight World War I, and it instituted its first peacetime draft in 1939 as war with the Nazis became likely. The World War II draft included the registration of women. During the late 1940s and early 1950s, men were required to spend two years on active duty, followed by time in the reserves.

FROM THE BENCH

Rostker v. *Goldberg*: Women and Draft Registration

In 1980, Congress reinstated draft registration but rejected President Carter's call to extend the requirement to women. The registration law revived a 1971 lawsuit brought by several men who alleged that a male-only draft was unconstitutional.

The case went up to the Supreme Court which held, in *Rostker* v. *Goldberg*, 453 U.S. 57 (1981), that it was constitutional to require men, but not women, to register. The vote was 6–3.

Justice William Rehnquist's majority opinion began by stating the principle that federal courts rarely second-guess the president and Congress in matters of national defense:

> This case arises in the context of Congress' authority over national defense and military affairs, and perhaps in no other area has the Court accorded Congress greater deference. In rejecting the registration of women, Congress explicitly relied upon its constitutional powers.

Turning to Congress's decision to limit draft registration to males, Rehnquist observed:

> The question of registering women for the draft not only received considerable national attention and was the subject of wide-ranging public debate, but also was extensively considered by Congress in hearings, floor debate, and in committee.

He also found that Congress had sound reasons for a male-only registration requirement:

> The restrictions on the participation of women in combat in the Navy and Air Force are [imposed by federal law]....The Army and Marine Corps preclude the use of women in combat as a matter of established policy....
>
> The existence of the combat restrictions clearly indicates the basis for Congress' decision to exempt women for registration. The purpose of registration was to prepare for a draft of combat troops. Since women are excluded from combat, Congress concluded that they would not be needed in the event of a draft, and decided not to register them.

Rehnquist next concluded that Congress could treat men and women differently in a draft:

> This is not a case of Congress arbitrarily choosing to burden one of two similarly situated groups, such as would be the case with an all-black or all-white, or an all-Catholic or all-Lutheran, or an all-Republican or all-Democratic registration. Men and women, because of the combat restrictions on women, are simply not similarly situated for purposes of a draft or registration for a draft.

Justice Byron White dissented. Although he believed it was constitutional to exclude women from combat, he found that Congress had anticipated that it might someday have to draft women for noncombat positions. That being the case, he found that limiting registration to men was unconstitutional.

Justice Thurgood Marshall also dissented. He, too, agreed that it would be constitutional to exclude women from combat and to draft more men than women. However, he found it inconsistent for Congress on one hand to encourage women to serve, but on the other hand to conclude that they could not be drafted. Even assuming that banning women from combat was "an important governmental interest" justifying different treatment of the sexes, Marshall argued that excluding women from registration was not "substantially related" to that goal. He disagreed with the assumption that all draftees would be combat ready, noting that the Pentagon had indicated that draftees could be needed for support positions that could be filled by women. If female draftees could perform as well as male draftees, he saw no military need to exclude them from the draft. Marshall also rejected the majority's conclusion that drafting a limited number of women would impair military flexibility. Though he conceded that drafting "very large numbers" of women would be disruptive, he found no justification for excluding *all* women from the draft by refusing to register them in the first place.

Under today's policy, although women do not have to register, the Selective Service System has a standby plan under which health-care professionals— including women—would be drafted should the military experience a severe shortage of these individuals.

(Continued from page 101)

the sexes are equal under the law. Even though the law generally requires equal treatment for women, many draw the line at forcing them into battle. With polls showing Americans equally divided on the issue, any decision on drafting women is certain to cause a backlash. Feminists would consider a male-only draft a step back toward second-class status for women; supporters of traditional gender roles would object strenuously to sending women, especially wives and mothers, into battle.

> • **Has the law done enough to treat the sexes equally? Or have we gone too far?**

Another issue that could divide Americans is whether gays should be drafted. Federal law calls for the discharge of gay men and lesbians from the armed services, although President Clinton's "don't ask, don't tell" policy has softened the ban, allowing gays to serve as long as they do not call attention to their homosexuality. A return of the draft, however, would put the military in a bind: If it stuck to the current policy, draftees might try to avoid serving by claiming to be gay; if it lifted the ban, there could be resentment toward, and possible mistreatment of, gay soldiers.

Reviving the draft also would reopen the issue of conscientious objection. In *United States* v. *Seeger*, 380 U.S. 163 (1965), the Supreme Court adopted what many consider a liberal standard: Even if a man did not belong to a church, he could claim conscientious-objector status if his antiwar beliefs were sincere and meaningful, and occupied a place in his life parallel to that filled by God in a churchgoer's belief system. Some experts think the *Seeger* standard is so inclusive that any man wishing to opt out of combat would be allowed to do so. If that were to happen, the government would have to set up an elaborate civilian work program, and the Selective Service System would be forced to call up thousands of additional men to make up for those excused from combat.

> • **Should conscientious objectors be opposed to all wars, or is it enough that they oppose a specific war?**

A Look at Draft/National Service Proposals

Although neither a draft nor a national service requirement is likely in the near future, there has been considerable debate about the issue. Both scholars and lawmakers have offered proposals for discussion. While all would require at least some young people to serve, there are differences in the details: whether women as well as men must serve, what the length of service would be, and whether military service would be part of the obligation. The better-known proposals include the following:

- **Bayh/McCain.** In 2001, Senators Evan Bayh, a Democrat from Indiana, and John McCain, a Republican from Arizona, introduced the Call to Service Act.[79] Their bill would create a new, short-term enlistment option. Under their "18-18-18" plan, one could qualify for an $18,000 bonus, in addition to regular pay, after 18 months' active and 18 months' reserve duty. The bill also would increase Ameri-Corps enrollment to 250,000 per year, with half its members assisting in homeland defense. McCain, in particular, makes no secret of his desire to make national service mandatory, but he realizes it is politically unfeasible at this time.

- **Should the money spent on AmeriCorps be given to private charities instead?**

- **Morris Janowitz.** Professor Janowitz of the University of Chicago proposes a mandatory national service program for men, combined with a selective draft. His plan would require a man turning 18 to choose whether to enlist in the military, take his chances in a draft lottery and do civilian work if not chosen, or apply for conscientious-objector status. Deferments would be kept to a minimum. Men chosen in the lottery would enter the military at age 19; those not chosen would have until age 26 to finish their civilian service.[80]

- **Should draftees have the option of choosing civilian service?**

- **David Hackworth.** Colonel Hackworth, a highly decorated veteran and military-affairs commentator, proposes universal military training for both sexes. Under his proposal, Americans turning 18 would take six months of military basic training, followed by a year of civilian service in a field such as law enforcement or health care. Those who opt for a longer tour of duty in the military would qualify for GI Bill benefits. Hackworth is especially concerned that young people are physically and morally "soft": "[M]ore than 60 percent—almost twice the WWII rejection level— of young males couldn't make it into the service in 1999 because of poor condition, past drug use or past trouble at school or with the law."[81]

- **Charles Moskos.** Professor Moskos of the University of Chicago proposes a military draft for men only. The tour of active duty would be short—he suggests 18 months—with draftees being assigned to work such as peacekeeping duty, and would be followed by a two-year reserve commitment. His proposal calls for "generous" alternative civilian service options. Moskos proposes starting conscription at the top of the social ladder, beginning with the graduates of leading universities. He asks: "Who better to do a term of service than those who benefit most?"[82]

- **Rangel/Conyers.** In 2003, Democratic Representatives Charles Rangel of New York and John Conyers of Michigan introduced a bill that would extend draft registration to women and require all young Americans to perform two years' service.[83] Their plan would authorize the president to use a draft, as necessary, to fill military manpower needs. Those not drafted would have to perform civilian service by age 26. Exemptions would be limited to extreme hardship or physical or mental disability.

- **Should military training be part of a national service program?**

- **Smith/Weldon**. After the September 11 attacks, Republican Representatives Nick Smith of Michigan and Kurt Weldon of Pennsylvania introduced a bill that would require universal military training for men and would give women the option of volunteering.[84] The six- to 12-month obligation would begin with military basic training, vocational training, and courses in history, international relations, and military tactics. A military tour of duty or a civilian homeland-security assignment would follow. According to Smith, "Going through the discipline of a 'boot camp' environment with physical fitness and some hands-on vocational training would benefit many young men."[85]

Present-day Americans take the all-volunteer military for granted, just as earlier generations saw the draft as an inevitable part of a man's life. Although few expect conscription to return soon, the world is becoming more dangerous. Conflict overseas, or more terror attacks at home, could strain the military and create pressure to bring back the draft. Although the public currently opposes the draft, it was once very popular and might become so again. In the meantime, some Americans, including members of Congress, have offered proposals that would require young people to serve their country in some manner. Even if none of those proposals becomes law, the issue of mandatory service will be debated for years to come.

The History of the Draft

1. Gary Hart, *The Minuteman: Restoring an Army of the People.* New York: The Free Press, 1998, p. 21.
2. *Selective Draft Law Cases,* 245 U.S. 366, 380 (1918).
3. John Franklin Leach, *Conscription in the United States: Historical Background.* Rutland, VT: Charles E. Tuttle Publishing Co., 1952, p. 38.
4. U.S. Constitution, Article I, §8, cl. 12, 15.
5. John Remington Graham, *Draft by What Authority? A Constitutional History of the Military Draft.* Minneapolis, MN: Ross & Haines, Inc., 1971, p. 29.
6. Leach, p. 454.
7. James Burk, "The Military Obligation of Citizens Since Vietnam," *Parameters* 31(2), (Summer 2001), pp. 48–60.
8. Ibid.
9. U.S. Undersecretary of Defense, *Conscription Threatens Hard-Won Achievements and Military Readiness.* Washington, D.C.: U.S. Defense Department, 2003, p. 9. Available online at *http://www.defenselink.mil/news/Jan2003/d20030114avf.pdf.*

Point: An All-Volunteer Military Endangers National Security

10. Office of the President of the United States, *The National Security Strategy of the United States of America.* Washington, D.C.: Office of the President of the United States, 2002, p. 29.
11. Charles Moskos and Paul Glastris, "Now Do You Believe We Need a Draft?" *Washington Monthly Online,* November 2001. Available online at *http://www.washingtonmonthly.com/features/2001/0111.moskos.glastris.html.*
12. Phyllis Schlafly, "The Feminization of the U.S. Military," 1999. Available online at *http://www.eagleforum.org/column/1999/aug99/99_08_11.html.*
13. Charles Moskos, "Reviving the Citizen-Solider," *The Public Interest* 147 (Spring 2002), pp. 76–85.
14. Gary Hart, *The Minuteman: Restoring an Army of the People.* New York: The Free Press, 1998, p. 171.

15. Charles Moskos, *A Call to Civic Service: National Service for Country and Community.* New York: The Free Press, 1988, p. 19.
16. John McCain, "Putting the National in National Service," *Washington Monthly* 33(10), (October 2001), p. 14.
17. Ibid.
18. Charles Rangel, "Bring Back the Draft," Op-Ed, *The New York Times,* December 31, 2002.
19. David H. Hackworth, "Will Osama bin Laden Bring Back the Draft?" *Soldiers for the Truth Weekly Newsletter,* February 20, 2002. Available online at *http://www.sftt.org/dw02202002.html.*

Counterpoint: The United States Can Meet Its Military Needs Without a Draft

20. Doug Bandow, "Fighting the War Against Terrorism: Elite Forces, Yes; Conscripts, No," *Cato Institute Policy Analysis* No. 430 (April 10, 2002), p. 1. Available online at *http://www.cato.org/pubs/pas/pa-430es.html.*
21. United States Undersecretary of Defense, *Conscription Threatens Hard-Won Achievements and Military Readiness.* Washington, D.C.: U.S. Department of Defense, p. 4. Available online at *http://www.defenselink.mil/news/Jan2003/d20030114avf.pdf.*
22. United States Department of Defense, News Transcript: DoD News Briefing— Secretary Rumsfeld and General Myers, January 13, 2003, p. 8. Available online at *http://www.defenselink.mil/news/Jan2003/t01072003_t0107sd.html.*
23. "Military Draft Now Part of Past," *The Washington Times,* December 31, 2000.
24. Bandow, p. 1.
25. United States Undersecretary of Defense, p. 4.
26. United States Department of Defense, News Transcript: Background Briefing on the All-Volunteer Force, January 13, 2003. Available online at *http://www.defenselink.mil/news/Jan2003/t01132003_t113bkgd.html.*
27. Bandow, p. 3.

28 Keith B. Hauk and Greg H. Parlier, "Recruiting: Crisis and Cures," *Command & General Staff College Military Review* 73 (May–June 2000), p. 4. Available online at *http://cgsc.leavenworth.army.mil/milrev/english/MayJun00/hauk.asp.*

29 Doug Bandow, "Fixing What Ain't Broke," *Cato Institute Policy Analysis* No. 350 (August 31, 1999), p. 18. Available online at *http://www.cato.org/pubs/pas/pa351-no-appendix.pdf.*

30 United States Undersecretary of Defense, p. 4.

31 James Burk, "The Military Obligation of Citizens Since Vietnam," *Parameters* 31(2) (Summer 2001), pp. 48–60.

Point: Reviving the Draft Would Benefit Society

32 Charles Moskos, *A Call to Civic Service: National Service for Country and Community.* New York: The Free Press, 1988, p. 135.

33 Keith B. Hauk and Gregg Parlier, "Recruiting: Crisis and Cures," *Command & General Staff College Military Review* 73 (May–June 2000), p. 3.

34 Democratic Leadership Council. Citizenship and National Service, Chapter 2, 1988. Available online at *http://www.ndol.org/ndol_ci.cfm?contentid=250403&kaid=115&subid=145.*

35 "Military Mirrors Working-Class America," *The New York Times*, March 30, 2003.

36 Moskos, p. 144.

37 Democratic Leadership Council, 1988.

38 Stephen Ambrose, "The End of the Draft, and More," *National Review* 51(15) (August 9, 1999), p. 35.

39 David Hackworth, "Time to Return to the Citizen Soldier," December 27, 1994. Available online at *http://www.hackworth.com/27dec94.html.*

40 Charles Moskos and Paul Glastris, "Now Do You Believe We Need a Draft?" *Washington Monthly* (November 2001).

41 Stanley Kurtz, "Revive the Draft: Time for Some Serious Preparations," *National Review Online*, September 12, 2001. Available online at *http://www.nationalreview.com/contributors/kurtzprint091201.html.*

42 James Burk, "The Military Obligation of Citizens Since Vietnam," *Parameters* 31(2), 2001, pp. 48–60.

43 Gary Hart, *The Minuteman: Restoring an Army of the People.* New York: The Free Press, 1998, p. 132.

Counterpoint: Reviving the Draft Would Do More Harm Than Good

44 "Military Draft Now Part of Past," *Washington Times*, December 31, 2000.

45 United States Undersecretary of Defense, *Conscription Threatens Hard-Won Achievements and Military Readiness.* Washington, D.C.: U.S. Department of Defense, p. 5. Available online at *http://www.defenselink.mil/news/Jan2003/d20030114avf.pdf.*

46 Milton Friedman, "Why Not a Voluntary Army?" in Sol Tax, ed., *The Draft: A Handbook of Facts and Alternatives.* Chicago: University of Chicago, 1967, p. 201.

47 United States Department of Defense, News Transcript: DoD News Briefing— Secretary Rumsfeld and General Myers, January 13, 2003, p. 8. Available online at *http://www.defenselink.mil/news/Jan2003/t01072003_t0107sd.html.*

48 Ibid.

49 President's Commission on an All-Volunteer Armed Force, *The Report of the President's Commission on an All-Volunteer Armed Force.* New York: The Macmillan Company, 1970, p. 32.

50 Doug Bandow, "Fixing What Ain't Broke," *Cato Institute Policy Analysis* No. 350 (August 31, 1999), p. 9. Available online at *http://www.cato.org/pubs/pas/pa351-no-appendix.pdf.*

51 Thomas G. Moore, "How to Reduce Terrorism: Bring American Troops Home," Op-Ed, *San Jose Mercury-News*, June 11, 2002.

52 Doug Bandow, "Fighting the War Against Terrorism: Elite Forces, Yes; Conscripts, No," *Cato Institute Policy Analysis* No. 430 (April 10, 2002), p. 1. Available online at *http://www.cato.org/pubs/pas/pa-430es.html.*

53 News Release, Office of U.S. Representative Ron Paul, "Paul Introduces Legislation Opposing Military Conscription," March 26, 2002. Available online at *http://www.house.gov/paul/press/ press2002/pr032802.htm.*

54 Bruce Chapman, "A Bad Idea, Whose Time is Past: The Case Against National Service," *Brookings Review* 20(4) (Fall 2002), pp. 10–13.

55 Robert Higgs, "War and Leviathan in Twentieth-Century America: Conscription as the Keystone," 1996. Available online at *http://www.independent.org/tii/news/ 960400Higgs.html.*

Point: Even Without a Draft, a National Service Requirement Would Benefit Society

56 Democratic Leadership Council. Citizenship and National Service, Chapter 2, 1988. Available online at *http://www.ndol.org/ndol_ci.cfm?con-tentid=250403&kaid=115&subid=145.*

57 Robert Litan, "September 11, 2001: The Case for Universal Service," *Brookings Review* 20(4) (Fall 2002), pp. 6–9.

58 Ibid.

59 "Making Americans: New Push for National Service; Sept. 11 Revives Interest in Citizenship Duty for Youth," *San Francisco Chronicle*, January 6, 2002. Available online at *http://www.americorpsalums.org/ newstand/documentation/01062002.html.*

60 William James, "The Moral Equivalent of War," 1906. Available online at *http://www.emory.edu/EDUCATION/mfp/ moral.html.*

61 Philip Keisling, "Make National Service Mandatory for All," *Washington Monthly* 26 (January–February 1994), p. 43.

62 Morris Janowitz, "American Democracy and Military Service," *Society* 35(2) (January–February 1998), pp. 39–48.

63 William F. Buckley, *Gratitude: Reflections on What We Owe to Our Country.* New York: Random House, Inc., 1990, p. 51.

64 John McCain, "Putting the National in National Service," *Washington Monthly* 33(10) (October 2001), p. 14.

65 Buckley, p. 152.

Counterpoint: A National Service Requirement Is Unnecessary and Unfair

66 Bruce Chapman, "A Bad Idea, Whose Time is Past: The Case Against National Service," *Brookings Review* 20(4) (Fall 2002), pp. 10–13.

67 Doug Bandow, "Fighting the War Against Terrorism: Elite Forces, Yes; Conscripts, No," *Cato Institute Policy Analysis* No. 430 (April 10, 2002), p. 1. Available online at *http://www.cato.org/pubs/ pas/pa-430es.html.*

68 E.J. Dionne and Kayla Meltzer Drogosz, "United We Serve? The Debate Over National Service," *Brookings Review* 20(4) (Fall 2002), p. 2.

69 Bandow, p. 1.

70 Douglas Hicks, "Paved With Good Intentions: The Politics of National Service," *Christian Century*, 119(16) (July 31, 2002), p. 10.

71 Chapman, pp. 10–13.

72 Tod Lindberg, "Service and the State: Politicizing the Need for Social Connection," *Brookings Review* 20(4) (Fall 2002), pp. 38–41.

73 Chapman, pp. 10–13.

74 President's Commission on an All-Volunteer Force, *The Report of the President's Commission on an All-Volunteer Armed Force.* New York: The Macmillan Company, 1970, pp. 170–171.

75 William F. Buckley, *Gratitude: Reflections on What We Owe to Our Country.* New York: Random House, Inc., 1990, p. 113.

The Future of Mandatory Service

76 Gary Hart, *The Minuteman: Restoring an Army of the People.* New York: The Free Press, 1998, p. 75.

77 E.J. Dionne and Kayla Meltzer Drogosz, "United We Serve? The Debate Over National Service," *Brookings Review* 20(4) (Fall 2002), p. 2.

78 Ellen Goodman, "Chivalry Shouldn't Extend to the Draft," 2003. Available online at *http://www.postwritersgroup.com/ archives/good0114.htm.*

79 Senate Bill 1792, 107th Congress. Available online at *http://thomas.loc.gov/cgi-bin/query/z?c107:S.1792:*.

80 Morris Janowitz, "American Democracy and Military Service," *Society* 35(2) (January–February 1998), pp. 39–48.

81 David Hackworth, "Harry Truman Had it Right," 1999. Available online at *http://www.hackworth.com/8sep99.html*.

82 Charles Moskos, n.d. "Pro/Con Discussion Series: Should the United States Reinstate the Draft?" Available online from the Military Officers Association of America at *http://www.troa.org/forums/procon.asp?id=8*.

83 House Resolution 163, 107th Congress. Available online at *http://thomas.loc.gov/cgi-bin/query/z?c108:H.R.163:*.

84 House Resolution 3598, 106th Congress. Available online at *http://thomas.loc.gov/cgi-bin/query/z?c107:H.R.3598:*.

85 News Release, Office of U.S. Representative Nick Smith, "Smith Introduces National Service Bill," January 29, 2002. Available online at *http://www.house.gov/nicksmith/pr20129a_print.htm*.

Against Mandatory Service

Books and Articles

Bandow, Doug. "Fighting the War Against Terrorism: Elite Forces, Yes; Conscripts, No," *Cato Institute Policy Analysis No. 430*, 1 (April 10, 2002). Available online at *http://www.cato.org/pubs/pas/pa-430es.html*
————. "Fixing What Ain't Broke" *Cato Institute Policy Analysis No. 350*, 18 (August 31, 1999). Available online at *http://www.cato.org/pubs/pas/pa351-no-appendix.pdf.*
Friedman, Milton. "Why Not a Voluntary Army?" In Sol Tax, ed. *The Draft: A Handbook of Facts and Alternatives.* Chicago: University of Chicago, 1967.
National Advisory Commission on Selective Service. *In Pursuit of Equity: Who Serves When Not All Serve? Report of the National Advisory Commission on Selective Service.* Washington, D.C.: U.S. Government Printing Office, 1967.
President's Commission on an All-Volunteer Armed Force. *The Report of the President's Commission on an All-Volunteer Armed Force.* New York: The Macmillan Company, 1970.
U.S. Undersecretary of Defense. *Conscription Threatens Hard-Won Achievements and Military Readiness.* Washington, D.C.: U.S. Defense Department, 2003. Available online at *http://www.defenselink.mil/news/Jan2003/d20030114avf.pdf.*

Web Sites

Cato Institute*: *http://www.cato.org*
Nonprofit public policy research center that seeks to bring the public into the debate on the proper role of the government.

David Hackworth: *http://www.hackworth.com*
Website of author and soldier who writes in support of the idea that U.S. soldiers should not be deployed without appropriate training and for appropriate purposes.

Independent Institute*: *http://www.independent.org*
Analyzes public policy and researches possible new directions for the government to consider.

Libertarian Party: *http://www.lp.org*
Political party devoted to individual liberty, free-market economics, and a non-interventionist foreign policy.

Congressman Ron Paul (R-TX): *http://www.house.gov/paul*
The congressman from Texas is known as a champion of individual liberty and a limited constitutional government.

U.S. Department of Defense: *http://www.defenselink.mil*
The official site of the government agency with the primary responsibility for creating and implementing military policy.

In Favor of Mandatory Service

Books and Articles

Buckley, William F. *Gratitude: Reflections on What We Owe to Our Country.* New York: Random House, Inc., 1990.

Hart, Gary. *The Minuteman: Restoring an Army of the People.* New York: The Free Press, 1998.

James, William. "The Moral Equivalent of War." 1906. Available online at *http://www.constitution.org/wj/meow.htm.*

Moskos, Charles. *A Call to Civic Service: National Service for Country and Community.* New York: The Free Press, 1988.

Web Sites

Brookings Institution*: *http://www.brook.edu*
A nonprofit organization that researches ways to improve the effectiveness of government institutions and policy.

Democratic Leadership Council. *http://www.ndol.org*
National advocate group for a new, progressive public policy.

National Review*: *http://www.nationalreview.com*
A conservative magazine that examines political issues, including military policy.

Selective Service System: *http://www.sss.gov*
The official government agency that operates the registration system for the draft and provides troops when needed by the regular armed forces.

Washington Monthly*: *http://www.washingtonmonthly.com*
Online periodical that studies government action and presents ideas for solving problems of American society.

* The organization itself has not taken an official position on the draft or national service, but one or more spokespersons have posted material on that subject on the organization's web site.

Cases and Statutes

Rostker* v. *Goldberg, 453 U.S. 57 (1981)
> The Supreme Court held that it was constitutional to exclude women from the Selective Service registration process.

Selective Draft Law Cases, 245 U.S. 366 (1918)
> The Supreme Court said that Congress had the power under the Constitution to draft citizens for military service.

United States* v. *O'Brien, 391 U.S. 367 (1968)
> O'Brien's contention that the First Amendment gave him the right to burn his draft card was rejected on the grounds that Congress had a vital interest in the prevention of draft-card destruction.

United States* v. *Seeger, 380 U.S. 163 (1965)
> The Supreme Court held that Selective Service could not distinguish among different religious beliefs when determining who was eligible for conscientious-objector status.

Selective Service Act, 50 U.S. Code App. §§451 and following
> Establishes a system for the registration of male U.S. citizens, and certain non-citizens living in the United States, for a possible military draft. Resumption of the draft requires an act of Congress.

Concepts and Standards

all-volunteer military
citizen-soldier
militia
selective service
conscientious-objector status
deferments
"Total Force"
conscription
universal military training
"chicken hawks"
GI Bill
"warrior caste"
"underclass army"
national service
civic society
"federalized volunteerism"

Beginning Legal Research

The goal of POINT/COUNTERPOINT is not only to provide the reader with an introduction to a controversial issue affecting society, but also to encourage the reader to explore the issue more fully. This appendix, then, is meant to serve as a guide to the reader in researching the current state of the law as well as exploring some of the public-policy arguments as to why existing laws should be changed or new laws are needed.

Like many types of research, legal research has become much faster and more accessible with the invention of the Internet. This appendix discusses some of the best starting points, but of course "surfing the Net" will uncover endless additional sources of information—some more reliable than others. Some important sources of law are not yet available on the Internet, but these can generally be found at the larger public and university libraries. Librarians usually are happy to point patrons in the right direction.

The most important source of law in the United States is the Constitution. Originally enacted in 1787, the Constitution outlines the structure of our federal government and sets limits on the types of laws that the federal government and state governments can pass. Through the centuries, a number of amendments have been added to or changed in the Constitution, most notably the first ten amendments, known collectively as the Bill of Rights, which guarantee important civil liberties. Each state also has its own constitution, many of which are similar to the U.S. Constitution. It is important to be familiar with the U.S. Constitution because so many of our laws are affected by its requirements. State constitutions often provide protections of individual rights that are even stronger than those set forth in the U.S. Constitution.

Within the guidelines of the U.S. Constitution, Congress—both the House of Representatives and the Senate—passes bills that are either vetoed or signed into law by the President. After the passage of the law, it becomes part of the United States Code, which is the official compilation of federal laws. The state legislatures use a similar process, in which bills become law when signed by the state's governor. Each state has its own official set of laws, some of which are published by the state and some of which are published by commercial publishers. The U.S. Code and the state codes are an important source of legal research; generally, legislators make efforts to make the language of the law as clear as possible.

However, reading the text of a federal or state law generally provides only part of the picture. In the American system of government, after the

116

legislature passes laws and the executive (U.S. President or state governor) signs them, it is up to the judicial branch of the government, the court system, to interpret the laws and decide whether they violate any provision of the Constitution. At the state level, each state's supreme court has the ultimate authority in determining what a law means and whether or not it violates the state constitution. However, the federal courts—headed by the U.S. Supreme Court—can review state laws and court decisions to determine whether they violate federal laws or the U.S. Constitution. For example, a state court may find that a particular criminal law is valid under the state's constitution, but a federal court may then review the state court's decision and determine that the law is invalid under the U.S. Constitution.

It is important, then, to read court decisions when doing legal research. The Constitution uses language that is intentionally very general—for example, prohibiting "unreasonable searches and seizures" by the police—and court cases often provide more guidance. For example, the U.S. Supreme Court's 2001 decision in *Kyllo* v. *United States* held that scanning the outside of a person's house using a heat sensor to determine whether the person is growing marijuana is unreasonable—*if* it is done without a search warrant secured from a judge. Supreme Court decisions provide the most definitive explanation of the law of the land, and it is therefore important to include these in research. Often, when the Supreme Court has not decided a case on a particular issue, a decision by a federal appeals court or a state supreme court can provide guidance; but just as laws and constitutions can vary from state to state, so can federal courts be split on a particular interpretation of federal law or the U.S. Constitution. For example, federal appeals courts in Louisiana and California may reach opposite conclusions in similar cases.

Lawyers and courts refer to statutes and court decisions through a formal system of citations. Use of these citations reveals which court made the decision (or which legislature passed the statute) and when and enables the reader to locate the statute or court case quickly in a law library. For example, the legendary Supreme Court case *Brown* v. *Board of Education* has the legal citation 347 U.S. 483 (1954). At a law library, this 1954 decision can be found on page 483 of volume 347 of the U.S. Reports, the official collection of the Supreme Court's decisions. Citations can also be helpful in locating court cases on the Internet.

Understanding the current state of the law leads only to a partial under-standing of the issues covered by the POINT/COUNTERPOINT series. For a fuller understanding of the issues, it is necessary to look at public-policy arguments that the current state of the law is not adequately addressing the issue. Many groups lobby for new legislation or changes to existing legislation; the National Rifle Association (NRA), for example, lobbies Congress and the state legislatures constantly to make existing gun control laws less restrictive and not to pass additional laws. The NRA and other groups dedicated to various causes might also intervene in pending court cases: a group such as Planned Parenthood might file a brief *amicus curiae* (as "a friend of the court")—called an "amicus brief"—in a lawsuit that could affect abortion rights. Interest groups also use the media to influence public opinion, issuing press releases and frequently appearing in interviews on news programs and talk shows. The books in POINT/COUNTERPOINT list some of the interest groups that are active in the issue at hand, but in each case there are countless other groups working at the local, state, and national levels. It is important to read everything with a critical eye, for sometimes interest groups present information in a way that can be read only to their advantage. The informed reader must always look for bias.

Finding sources of legal information on the Internet is relatively simple thanks to "portal" sites such as FindLaw (*www.findlaw.com*), which provides access to a variety of constitutions, statutes, court opinions, law review articles, news articles, and other resources—including all Supreme Court decisions issued since 1893. Other useful sources of information include the U.S. Government Printing Office (*www.gpo.gov*), which contains a complete copy of the U.S. Code, and the Library of Congress's THOMAS system (*thomas.loc.gov*), which offers access to bills pending before Congress as well as recently passed laws. Of course, the Internet changes every second of every day, so it is best to do some independent searching. Most cases, studies, and opinions that are cited or referred to in public debate can be found online— and *everything* can be found in one library or another.

The Internet can provide a basic understanding of most important legal issues, but not all sources can be found there. To find some documents it is necessary to visit the law library of a university or a public law library; some cities have public law libraries, and many library systems keep legal documents at the main branch. On the following page are some common citation forms.

COMMON CITATION FORMS

Source of Law	Sample Citation	Notes
U.S. Supreme Court	*Employment Division* v. *Smith*, 485 U.S. 660 (1988)	The U.S. Reports is the official record of Supreme Court decisions. There is also an unofficial Supreme Court ("S.Ct.") reporter.
U.S. Court of Appeals	*United States* v. *Lambert,* 695 F.2d 536 (11th Cir.1983)	Appellate cases appear in the Federal Reporter, designated by "F." The 11th Circuit has jurisdiction in Alabama, Florida, and Georgia.
U.S. District Court	*Carillon Importers, Ltd.* v. *Frank Pesce Group, Inc.*, 913 F.Supp. 1559 (S.D.Fla.1996)	Federal trial-level decisions are reported in the Federal Supplement ("F.Supp."). Some states have multiple federal districts; this case originated in the Southern District of Florida.
U.S. Code	Thomas Jefferson Commemoration Commission Act, 36 U.S.C., §149 (2002)	Sometimes the popular names of legislation—names with which the public may be familiar—are included with the U.S. Code citation.
State Supreme Court	*Sterling* v. *Cupp*, 290 Ore. 611, 614, 625 P.2d 123, 126 (1981)	The Oregon Supreme Court decision is reported in both the state's reporter and the Pacific regional reporter.
State statute	Pennsylvania Abortion Control Act of 1982, 18 Pa. Cons. Stat. 3203-3220 (1990)	States use many different citation formats for their statutes.

abolitionists, 8
abortion, 8
Afghanistan, 20, 27, 37
Algeria, 68
Al Qaeda, 23
Ambrose, Stephen, 51, 53
American Civil War, 69
  antidraft protests during, 13
  the Confederacy in, 13–14, 25
  and the draft, 10, 13–14, 16, 24
  the Union in, 13–14
American Revolution, 11, 14, 51
AmeriCorps, 74, 83, 86, 88–89, 105

Bandow, Doug, 37, 45, 88
  on the draft, 40–41, 70, 86
Bayh, Evan
  and the Call to Service Act, 105
Berryman, Susan, 63
Black, Hugo, 71
Bosnia, 69, 97
Broder, David, 27
Brown v. *Board of Education*, 117
Buckley, William F.
  on national service, 81, 94
  on universal military training, 53
Burk, James, 46
Bush, George H.W.
  as president, 45–46, 79
Bush, George W.
  as president, 23

Call to Service Act, 105
Canada
  the draft in, 100
capital punishment, 6, 8
Carnegie Foundation, 79
Carter, Jimmy
  as president, 15, 20, 100, 102
Cato Institute, 37, 86
Chapman, Bruce, 70, 75, 90, 93
China, 46
  the draft in, 100
civic duty, 10, 48–49, 57–58, 69, 72–74, 76, 78–79, 82, 84, 92
Civilian Conservation Corp (CCC), 76
Civil War. *See* American Civil War
Clay, Cassius Marcellus, a.k.a. Muhammad Ali
  conscientious-objector case of, 66–67
Clay v. *United States*, 66–67
Clinton, William "Bill"
  as president, 32–33, 72, 104
Cohen, Eliot, 38, 61
Cold War, 15, 20, 27, 53, 97
Colombia, 97
Congress, U.S., 33, 52, 107, 116, 118
  military authority of, 12–18, 20, 24–25, 30, 39, 44, 54, 58–59, 71, 100–103, 114

conscientious objectors, 11, 18, 39, 43, 55, 62–63, 66–67, 104–105, 114
conscription, 22, 58, 70, 75, 86, 100, 106–107
Continental Army, 11
Continental Congress, 14
Conyers, John
  draft proposal of, 106
Costa Rica, 80

Danzig, Richard, 69
death penalty, 6
Defense Department, 15, 37, 40–41, 46, 60, 64–65, 96, 99–100
Democratic Leadership Council, 50–51, 72–73, 79, 82
Dionne, E.J., 87
Discovery Institute, 70, 85, 90
Douglas, William, 39, 67
draft
  during the Civil War, 10, 13–14
  criticisms of, 15, 28, 42, 52, 61–63, 69–71
  deferments to, 16, 18, 33, 43, 54, 56, 61–63
  economic consequences of, 70, 92–93
  future of, 92, 96–98, 104
  history of, 10–21, 102

and homosexuals,
104
law cases and,
14–15, 24–25, 39,
58–59, 66,
100–104, 114
lotteries of, 15–16,
31, 42, 54, 61, 105
in other countries,
100–101
in peacetime, 14, 16,
39, 75
points against,
36–47, 60–71,
84–95
points for, 22–35,
48–59, 72–83
proposals of,
105–107
protests of, 13,
18–19, 58–59,
66–68
during Vietnam
War, 9, 15, 18–19,
21, 45, 56, 58,
61–62, 65–68, 71,
80, 82, 91, 95, 98
and women,
100–104, 114
draft boards, 16, 42,
66
draft-law violators, 15,
58
Drogosz, Kayla
Meltzer, 87

Eagle Forum, 29
Eisenhower, Dwight
as president, 79
England, 11–13, 51,
97–98
the draft in, 101
Parliament, 25, 32

Flynn, George, 31

Ford, Gerald
as president, 15
France, 13, 68
the draft in, 100
revolution in, 100
Frazier, Joe, 67
Friedman, Milton
on the draft, 63, 70
free-market argu-
ment, 92–93, 98

Gates Commission, 92
recommendations
of, 19–20, 30, 65,
68, 94
General Accounting
Office, 74
Germany, 30, 70
the draft in,
100–101
GI Bill, 44, 74, 79–80,
82, 106
Goodman, Ellen, 101
Great Depression, 76
"Greatest Generation,"
79
Greece
the draft in, 10–11

Hackworth, David,
53–54
on the draft, 34
universal military
training proposal
of, 106
Hart, Gary, 32
on universal military
training, 53, 98
Hawkins, Gabe C., 52
Hershey, Lewis B.
and the Selective
Service system,
30–31
Hicks, Douglas, 89
Higgs, Robert, 70–71

Hitler, Adolf, 70, 94,
101
Holmes, Albert
conscientious-
objector case of, 39
Holmes v. United
States, 39
homeland security,
26–27, 69, 82–83,
86, 97–98, 100, 105,
107
Hoover Institution,
29, 56, 69, 92
Hussein, Saddam, 70,
97

Independent Institute,
70
Industrial Revolution,
36
Iraq, 33, 39, 45,
70–71, 97
U.S. war against, 20,
23, 26
Israel
military training in,
9, 22, 70, 101
Italy, 100

James, William, 78
"The Moral Equiva-
lent of War,"
72–75
Janowitz, Morris, 78
mandatory national
service proposal
of, 105
Japan
bombing of Pearl
Harbor, 16
Johns Hopkins
University, 38
Johnson, Lyndon
as president, 18, 42,
46, 68

Justice Department,
66–67

Keisling, Phil, 78
Kennedy, John F.
as president, 79
Koran, 67
Korean War, 18, 20,
33, 40
Kosovo, 69, 97
Kurtz, Stanley, 29, 56
Kuwait, 45
Kyllo v. *United States*,
117

legal research,
116–118
Library of Congress,
118
Lindbergh, Tod, 92
Litan, Robert, 74
on national service,
75–76

Madison, James
as president, 12, 14,
24
mandatory service.
See also National
Service Program
future of, 96–107
Marshall Commission,
15, 42
Marshall, Thurgood,
103
McCain, John, 33, 80
and the Call to
Service Act, 105
Mexican War, 12–13
Mexico, 80
militarism, 74–75
military deserters, 15
military, U.S., 34, 49,
54, 57–58, 81,
96–97

academies of, 65
all-volunteer force,
10, 12, 14–16,
18–20, 23, 28, 32,
35, 37–38, 40–42,
44, 46–48, 50, 60–
62, 65, 71, 80, 92,
107
critics of, 51, 62–63,
65
entry standards of,
49–50
homosexuals in, 104
racial segregation in,
15, 51–53
recruitment of, 9,
29–30, 35, 38, 43,
48, 54–55, 82, 93
roles of, 64, 69,
97–99
and women, 29,
100–104, 114
militia, 11–13, 16, 22
"Moral Equivalent of
War, The " (William
James), 72, 74–75
Moore, Thomas Gale,
69
Moskos, Charles, 27,
32, 49, 51, 56, 98
draft proposal of,
106

National Guard and
Reserves, 15–16, 18,
21, 30, 38, 43, 46, 65,
97
National Rifle Associ-
ation (NRA), 118
national service pro-
gram, 72–96
advocates of, 73, 77,
81–84, 88, 90, 94
costs of, 73–74,
84–85, 95

deferments to, 82
as draft alternative,
72–73
opponents of,
84–86, 89–91, 93
proposals of,
105–107
services provided by,
73, 82, 86, 93
Nation of Islam, 66
Nazi regime, 16, 70, 101
New York City
antidraft protests in,
13
New York Times, The,
49
Nixon, Richard
as president, 14, 18,
31, 46, 92
Nobel Prize, 92

O'Brien, David
draft protest case of,
58–59, 114
Operation Desert
Storm, 15, 20,
45–46

Palmer, John
McAuley, 32, 57
patriotism, 53, 86
Pearl Harbor, Hawaii
bombing of, 16, 56
Pennsylvania constitu-
tion, 12
Pentagon, 29, 41, 51,
60–61, 65–66, 68, 103
"total force" concept
of, 19–21
Prejean, Helen, 6
Presley, Elvis, 18

Rangel, Charles, 33
draft proposal of,
106

Reagan, Ronald
as president, 20, 70
Regimental Combat
Team, 422nd, 51
Rehnquist, William,
102–103
Reserve Officers
Training Corps
(ROTC), 62, 64
Rome
the draft in, 10–11,
57
Rotsker v. *Goldberg*,
15, 100–104, 114
Rumsfeld, Donald, 37
Russia, 46. *See also*
Soviet Union
the draft in, 101

Saving Private Ryan,
23
Schlafly, Phyllis, 29
Selective Draft Law
Cases, 14, 24–25,
114
Selective Service Act
(1917), 14, 16, 58,
66–67, 114
Selective Service system,
15, 17, 21, 30–31,
42, 52, 54–56,
58–59, 61–62,
103–104
Selective Service v.
Minnesota Public
Interest Research
Group, 15
Selective Training and
Service Act (1940),
14
September 11, 2001
terrorist attacks on,
9, 20, 23, 37, 56,
88, 97, 107
slavery, 8

Smith, Nick
universal military
training proposal
of, 107
Social Security, 76
Solomon Amendment
(1982), 15
Somalia, 32, 37
Soviet Union, 15, 18,
45, 96, 101. *See also*
Russia
invasion of
Afghanistan, 20
Spain, 100
Spanish-American
War, 14, 16
Stalin, Joseph, 94
Switzerland
military training in,
9, 22, 53

Taliban, 27, 37
Tonkin Gulf Resolution,
39
Truman, Harry
as president, 15, 17,
52
Tse-tung, Mao, 94
Tuskegee Airmen,
51–52

Uniform Militia Act
(1792), 14
United Nations, 55
United States, 9–10,
18, 21, 60, 73
foreign policy of,
34–35, 64, 69–70,
93, 97, 99
government of, 7,
12–13, 17, 25, 27,
56, 59, 71, 79–80,
82, 87, 95, 116
history of, 44, 66,
68, 72

threats on, 23
at war, 9–16, 18, 20,
23–28, 30–37, 39–
40, 51, 54–56, 60,
69, 72, 96–97
United States Air
Force, 102
United States Army,
40, 102
air corps of, 52
United States Code,
116, 118–19
United States Consti-
tution, 7–8, 25, 39,
114, 116–117
bill of rights in, 7,
116
first amendment to,
7, 114
framers of, 12, 14,
21, 24, 32, 98
second amendment
to, 7
thirteenth amend-
ment to, 25
United States Govern-
ment Printing
Office, 118
United States Marines,
26, 44, 102
United States Navy,
69, 102
United States
Supreme Court, 71,
117–119
interpretations of
the Constitution,
7–8, 14–15,
24–25, 39, 52, 58,
66–67, 100–104,
114
United States v.
O'Brien, 58, 114
United States v. *Seeger*,
104, 114

universal military training, 14, 22, 42, 53, 55, 61, 80, 101, 106–107
Universal Military Training and Service Act (1948), 15
University of Chicago, 92, 105–106

Vietnam War, 28, 31, 33, 37, 39–40, 54–55, 60, 72
and the draft, 9, 15, 18–19, 21, 45, 56, 58, 61–63, 65–68, 71, 80, 82, 91, 95, 98
protesters of, 18–19, 58, 66–68
Villa, Pancho, 30

War of 1812, 12, 14, 24
Warren, Earl, 58–59
Washington, George, 11–12, 14, 80
Weldon, Kurt
universal military training proposal of, 107

White, Byron, 103
White, Edward, 24–25
World Trade Center
terror attacks on, 20
World War I, 16–17, 24, 57, 69, 97, 100–101
World War II, 14, 18, 30, 37, 39, 51, 53, 55–56, 61, 79–80, 92, 97–98, 100–101, 106

Young, Andrew, 55

page:
17: Courtesy of the Library of Congress, LC-USZC4-9018
26: Photo by Lance Cpl. Brian L. Wickliffe, US Marine Corps/ Courtesy of US Department of Defense
40: Courtesy of US Department of Defense/Directorate for Information Operations and Reports
52: Associated Press, AP
64: Courtesy of US Department of Defense/Directorate for Information Operations and Reports
77: Courtesy of the Library of Congress, LC-USZC4-1588
86: Data compiled from 'A Profile of AmeriCorps Members at Baseline', June 2001
89: Data compiled from 'A Profile of AmeriCorps Members at Baseline', June 2001
99: Courtesy of US Department of Defense/© United States Government 2002

Cover: Cpl. Matthew J. Apprendi/US Marine Corps Official Photo Archive

PAUL RUSCHMANN, J.D., is a legal analyst and writer based in Canton, Michigan. He received his undergraduate degree from the University of Notre Dame and his law degree from the University of Michigan. He is a member of the State Bar of Michigan. His areas of specialization include legislation, public safety, traffic and transportation, and trade regulation. He is also the author of *Legalizing Marijuana*, another title in the POINT/COUNTERPOINT series. He can be found online at *www.PaulRuschmann.com.*

ALAN MARZILLI, of Durham, North Carolina, is an independent consultant working on several ongoing projects for state and federal government agencies and nonprofit organizations. He has spoken about mental health issues in more than 20 states, the District of Columbia, and Puerto Rico; his work includes training mental health administrators, nonprofit management and staff, and people with mental illness and their family members on a wide variety of topics, including effective advocacy, community-based mental health services, and housing. He has written several handbooks and training curricula that are used nationally. He managed statewide and national mental health advocacy programs and worked for several public interest lobbying organizations in Washington, D.C., while studying law at Georgetown University.